Invitatic
Persoı
Construct
Psychology

Second Edition

TREVOR BUTT and VIVIEN BURR
School of Human and Health Sciences,
University of Huddersfield

General Editor

Professor Windy Dryden
Goldsmiths College, University of London

W
WHURR PUBLISHERS
LONDON AND PHILADELPHIA

© 2004 Whurr Publishers

This edition first published 2004 by
Whurr Publishers Ltd
19b Compton Terrace, London N1 2UN, England
325 Chestnut Street, Philadelphia PA19106, USA

First edition published 1992

All rights reserved. No part of this publication may be
reproduced, stored in a retrieval system, or transmitted
in any form or by any means, electronic, mechanical,
photocopying, recording or otherwise, without the
prior permission of Whurr Publishers Limited.

This publication is sold subject to the conditions that it
shall not, by way of trade or otherwise, be lent, resold,
hired out, or otherwise circulated without the Publisher's
prior consent, in any form of binding or cover other than
that in which it is published, and without a similar condition including this condition being imposed upon any
subsequent purchaser.

British Library Cataloguing in Publication Data

A catalogue record for this book is available from the
British Library.

ISBN 1 86156 387 6

Printed and bound in the UK by Athenaeum Press Limited,
Gateshead, Tyne & Wear.

Contents

Preface to the second edition

Invitation to Personal Construct Psychology was written primarily for students. Introductory texts on personality theory often seem to provide a somewhat two-dimensional account of personal construct psychology, and we wanted it to come alive by focusing on what we hoped were engaging and accessible issues in everyday life. We aimed to capture the reader's interest by posing a series of silly questions, none which can be answered simply (our working title had been *Asking Silly Questions*). Each reflects what in Kellian terms is a poor bipolar construct, but constructs which are none the less commonly drawn on in our culture. Our point was that our thinking is imprisoned by our construing, and a re-examination of this construing is necessary for any psychological reconstruction. Our impression is that the book was generally well received, and it's gratifying that it has remained in print for 12 years.

Our aim had never been to provide a comprehensive introduction to the area, but an invitation; one that might interest the reader and encourage further reading. So our strategy had been to write informally and fluently in plain English, making the minimum of references. In reviewing this series of essays, our feeling is that they are still relevant and continue to reflect the way people think about their lives. So we've left most of them more or less untouched, although we have made minor modifications to our language and provided updated references where this seemed appropriate. However, we have also added one new essay: 'Am I traumatised?' This is because constructivist work on trauma and grief has grown considerably in the past decade, and we want to highlight this. Then the two essays on assessment and change in Part V also needed more attention. Personal construct psychology was devised within the tradition of American pragmatism; it was intended as a working theory that should help people to make sense of their lives. Its focus was in this psychological reconstruction, and essential to this is an assessment of construing. Part V thus centres on some major growth points in personal construct psychology. One of the most telling criticisms of the book was that it reproduced the fallacy in personality textbooks that not much had changed since Kelly's time and ignored much of the development and evolution in constructivist thought. So in the concluding essays we have updated and made reference to more contemporary work in the area.

In the paragraph above, we have referred to 'constructivism', a term we hardly used in the first edition. This is because of the way in which construct theory has developed in the past ten to 15 years. George Kelly died in 1967, but his theory has continued to evolve and contemporary scholars have elaborated its connections with other work in modern psychology. The umbrella term 'constructivism' underlines the common ground that many (who would not think of themselves exactly as Kellians) share with construct theorists. This is the assumption that the way we think, feel and act is not dictated by real and undisputable events as such, but by the way in which we interpret them. This results in a common view on how psychological reconstruction should be approached. Often, we are not in a position to simply change things or others, but we can work to change our constructions of them. When we are able to change the meaning we have of other people, we act towards them differently and open new possible ways of relating to them. Of course, psychological reconstruction does not have to mean consulting a therapist or a counsellor. We very much hope that this book contributes to extending this constructivist horizon for the reader.

Trevor Butt
Vivien Burr
Huddersfield, March 2004

Preface to the first edition

This book is concerned with the application of psychology to everyday life and is written primarily for anyone who is fascinated and puzzled by people (themselves included!). They may be engaged on a first course in psychology (for example a GCSE, 'A' level or degree course partly or wholly devoted to psychology) or simply an 'interested onlooker', and for this reason we use the absolute minimum of jargon and specialised language.

It is our experience that most people become interested in psychology because they wonder what makes people tick. They are alive with questions about the conduct of themselves and others. But disillusion often follows when they find that so much of academic psychology does not address these questions.

One argument they encounter is that they must learn to walk before they can run; there is a body of pure psychology that must be understood before it can be applied to anything. But the last thing you should try to do is to apply it to your own life! We have no sympathy with this argument. We believe that psychology should be readily applicable to people's daily experience. It should shed light on their dilemmas, problems and worries. Furthermore, we find the distinction between pure and applied psychology artificial. There is a constant interplay between the two and it is never too early to start looking at the psychology of everyday life. It is here that questions are posed and need answering and it is here that the usefulness of theories will be tested. It is a shame when theory is divorced from practice. A good theory is a useful theory.

One such good theory in the field of human affairs is George Kelly's Personal Construct Psychology (Kelly, 1955) (which will be referred to throughout as PCP), and this book constitutes an invitation to it. We say 'invitation' and not 'introduction' since we have not attempted a comprehensive account of the theory. We have tried to illustrate the spirit and some of the propositions of the theory in contexts which will be familiar to the reader. You are invited to try on a theoretical approach with no obligation to buy. Of course we hope that some of you will become interested enough to take a second look and read further.

This project arose out of conversations – conversations with students, friends and each other. Everyone is different, but at another level everyone is the same. We all have fears, aims, frustrations, dilemmas and self-defeating strategies. We often feel we are our own worst enemies and we have patterns of conduct we do not like – perhaps cannot even recognise – but feel powerless to change. And frequently human problems share a lowest common denominator: that we draw up our options in such a way that renders solution virtually impossible. We ask inappropriate questions and not surprisingly get inappropriate answers. We become the prisoners of our own patterns of thought.

We have chosen some common questions as the organising principle of this book. We have written a short essay on each, and try to shed light on the issues they raise and recommend a more useful reconstruction of the question. However, this is not a self-help book. Kellians have no simple recipe for how to live life, which is inevitably complicated and difficult. But any problem has to be framed appropriately before we can even begin to tackle it, and the process of reconstruction has to begin with a stroll around the psychological landscape in search of better perspectives.

Our reason for focusing on these questions is that they offer such a good vehicle for carrying PCP in a way that renders it digestible and understandable. Through them we attempt to spell out the theory as it applies to everyday life. One of Kelly's key concepts is that of 'range of convenience'. Any one of the questions that we commonly (and often implicitly) ask of our social world has a limited range of events to which it can sensibly be applied, and outside of this range it is useless or inappropriate. Nothing is more misleading than an inappropriate question that sounds, on the face of it, reasonable.

In an effort to underline the themes running through the questions we have chosen, we have organised them into five sections. Each deals with a central theme in PCP and is prefaced by a brief outline of what we consider to be the key issues.

Throughout the book we have made use of case studies which are fictional in that they never refer to a particular individual. They draw on common experiences and picture problems and dilemmas that we think people will find all too recognisable.

Chapter 1
Introduction

The aim of this introductory chapter is to help you to locate PCP on a kind of psychological 'map', so that you can understand how it stands in relation to other aspects of psychology. The chapter is divided into three parts, which broadly reflect the major issues dealt with in the rest of the book.

Psychology and the Nature of Knowledge

If you look for PCP in an introductory psychology textbook, you are likely to find it in the section on 'personality' (although, as we shall show, it is rather uneasily situated here). Typically, such a section would be a catalogue of contrasting theories, all attempting to offer some explanation for how you come to be the kind of person you are, and why individuals differ in their personality characteristics. Students are often confused by this plethora of explanations, and wonder how they are to decide which is 'the right one'. Freudianism, humanistic psychology, trait theories, behaviourism and personal construct psychology all seem convincing when you read about them, and students frequently end up watching their lecturers closely for clues as to the one he or she espouses, in an effort to answer the question.

But is it really sensible to ask which is the right one? Surely these great thinkers (with the exception of the 'right' one) cannot all be wrong? Must we really choose between them? An alternative is to question the whole idea of right and wrong when dealing with personality theories. After all, we naturally do this (though we may be unaware of it) when we think about a whole host of other things in our daily lives. I do not look at the desk at which I am writing and say 'Is this a nice piece of oak *or* a useful surface *or* a collection of atoms?'. It is (or can be thought of) as *all* of these things, depending on your perspective or what you want to do with it. They are different 'levels' of explanation for the same phenomenon. When the physicist asserts that the desk is ultimately a collection of tiny particles, he or she is not denying that it is either pleasing to the eye or useful to the writer. In the same way, we may think of a person as attractive, a seething mass of unconscious conflicts or an ingenious combination of carbon molecules. These are different constructions which we place upon the same phenomenon or event (in this case a person), and it makes no sense to ask which of these alternatives is correct. What *does* make sense is to ask which is the most useful construction for our current purposes.

George Kelly, the founder of PCP, makes this distinction between events and constructions. In dealing with the events of our daily lives, we bring to bear on them a potentially infinite range of constructions. Constructions cannot be judged in terms of their truth, their correctness, but only in terms of their usefulness. This belief is at the centre of PCP, and Kelly labelled it 'constructive alternativism'. We explore the nature of constructive alternativisrn more fully in Part I. As we shall see, it has important implications for our explanations of individual differences in psychology; but it also has implications beyond that, in how we think about the relationship between 'facts' and 'theories'.

Kelly contrasts constructive alternativism with what he referred to as 'accumulative fragmentalism'. These represent different philosophical positions in how knowledge advances: constructive alternativism holds that knowledge advances through the adoption of new perspectives, new frameworks (what Kuhn, the philosopher of science, calls paradigm shifts); this contrasts with the common-sense notion (accumulative fragmentalism), which implies that we become more knowledgeable as we collect more facts, more nuggets of truth. At first glance, it is all too easy to gain this impression of science, that most prestigious branch of knowledge, which can look like an impressive collection of facts, dispassionately observed. But in reality, scientists never go out and simply observe what is there; they are guided in what to look for by their theories. Theories tell us where to look. Facts do not lie about waiting to be picked up; they are visible only within the searchlight of a theory. Take for example a problem which occupied physicians of the nineteenth century – general paralysis of the insane (GPI). Before the development of microscopy, theories of cause focused on masturbation, but developments in theories about micro-organisms, coupled with technological advances, led to the question 'Is a micro-organism the cause of GPI?'. This in turn led to the finding that the syphilis spirochete is the cause of the condition. The question had to precede the finding. Scientific advance depends on the restructuring of questions, not the haphazard collection of facts.

As with science, so with our personal affairs. Many of the problems we face are due to our asking inappropriate questions. Kelly saw that people are like scientists in that their actions are guided by the theories they hold about themselves and those around them; the questions they are currently asking. These questions or theories are the person's bridge between their past and their future. They are shaped by experience, provide the framework for future action and are responsible for the particular anticipatory stance we take. They alert us to some events and blind us to others, 'Who is going to be the boss in this marriage?' is a question that one partner may be silently posing without realising that this is simply not an issue for the other. However, this won't stop the first partner from interpreting or construing the actions of the other in terms of their guiding question.

This brings us to the notion of good and bad questions. just as some theories are more useful than others in helping us to explain an event in physics or chemistry, so the theories with which we approach our personal world cannot be said to be true or untrue; some are more useful than others. *Good* questions give us answers we can use, some idea of what to do, how to deal with something, how to react to someone. *Bad* questions lead to unhelpful answers, they are simply not suited to the issues we face. 'Are you for me or against me?' might be useful in war or competitions, but in the context of most other interpersonal relationships it will lead to frustrating and restricted answers. *Bad* questions lead to people being stuck in unhelpful and demoralising cycles of experience.

Kelly insisted that if you want to help people to change, you must first understand the construction they are placing on their world, the theories they hold, and the questions they are asking. This leads us back to the issue of personality.

The Nature of Personality

The principle of constructive alternativism has two important implications for the concept of personality. First, it means that all the different theories of human nature that we encounter can be seen as different constructions, and our task is not to try to discover which is the 'correct' one, but to examine the usefulness of each in helping us to understand the nature of people. Second, it means that the clue to understanding a person lies in understanding their particular construction of the world. This is an issue on which we shall elaborate in Part II on personality and personal change. Our present aim is to say something about these constrasting views of human nature, to show both how they are similar to or different from each other, and how they contrast with PCP.

One reason why there are so many different kinds of theory in psychology is that, as in other disciplines, they arose at particular periods in history as a response to particular sets of problems. For example, Freud's psychoanalytic theory, in which he puts forward his own unique view of how people develop from childhood, grew out of his clinical practice. In fact one of the criticisms often levelled at Freud's theory is that it may have very little explanatory value outside the population on which it was based (the Austro-Hungarian middle class). A key feature of psychoanalytic theory is its emphasis upon the role of childhood experiences in later development. For Freud, the first few years of life are crucial in determining how a person is going to turn out, and he saw the child's relationships with its parents as of immense significance. Psychoanalytic theory is therefore 'deterministic' in that the experiences of early life set in motion a chain of psychological events resulting in a pattern of relationships which the person is powerless to change. The individual can be the victim of innate feelings of envy and hatred as well as of a bad early environment.

This is stating the case somewhat strongly, but serves to bring out the way in which PCP is essentially different from psychoanalytic constructions of human nature. PCP does not deny that a person's experiences can have a powerful impact upon the rest of their life, but Kelly insisted that it is not the event itself that has such force, but the way in which the person construes that event. It is the meaning that the person extracts from their experiences that is the important ingredient. PCP, too, grew out of one man's particular experience of trying to help others through psychotherapy. George Kelly was a therapist practising in the American Dust Bowl during the time of the depression. Among his clients were work-hardened farmers, living on the edge of poverty and deprivation. And yet what impressed Kelly was not how these people's experiences had damaged them psychologically but the way in which similar life-experiences were construed by one person in terms of hopelessness and helplessness and by another in terms of 'rising to the challenge' in the battle against adversity. It was the meaning that people saw in the events of their lives, Kelly found, which distinguished the troubled from the untroubled, and which directly informs their conduct, their behaviour.

Another contrast of PCP with psychoanalytic theory is to do with the agency of the individual. Whereas analysis characterises the person as the hapless victim of their childhood and innate forces, Kelly puts the person firmly in the driving seat of their own life, opening up possibilities for personal change which are difficult to reconcile with the Freudian view. In this, Kelly is perhaps typical of the more adventurous, romantic approaches to the person shown by American psychologists. His theory has a (some would say naive) flavour of 'you don't know what you can do until you try'. Reading him, you can easily imagine the wagons rolling into new frontier country where no one has gone before. By contrast, European theorists, perhaps shaped by their history, have taken a characteristic tragic or ironic view of the human predicament.

This determinism and lack of agency is not confined to psychoanalytic theory. Trait theories, like those of Cattell and Eysenck, share this feature, though their origins were markedly different from that of psychoanalysis. In the early twentieth century, workers such as Binet pioneered research on what is often referred to as 'individual differences'. The problems guiding such work were questions such as 'How do you sort out those children who would benefit from a certain kind of education?' and 'Which recruits should we train as aircrew?'. These questions naturally led to theories which located individuals along dimensions like 'intelligence' and 'extraversion'. Such dimensions imply that each of us has, as part of our psychological make-up, a certain amount of each of a number of these traits (Cattell, for example, thought that 16 such dimensions were sufficient to 'map out' the personality of any individual). Trait theory sees individuals as differing from each other in terms of how much of each trait they have, and individuals can be placed along any of these dimensions by measuring their traits through the use of tests and personality inventories. A key feature of most trait theories is that they see these traits as genetically endowed – we are born with them, just as we are born with the shape of our nose or the size of our feet. Environmental influences can of course have some impact on the final outcome (a boxer's nose may not turn out how nature intended) but by and large genetic factors are seen as more influential than environmental ones. In the case of personality, this means that the traits you are born with determine the kind of personality you will have when you grow up, and there isn't a great deal you can do about it. So we see again the qualities of determinism and lack of agency that are found in psychoanalytic approaches to personality, but which have no place in PCP.

We can see that personal change can have only a very limited role within these frameworks. But not all psychology conceptualises people as static and unchangeable; in fact, one of the most influential and, at the time, revolutionary approaches to the study of humankind focused on the malleability of behaviour – the behaviourist tradition. This too was a child of its time (the 1920s and 1930s) and was psychology's response to and emulation of the natural sciences, which were acquiring more and more prestige in the quest for knowledge. Observation, measurement and prediction of behaviour were at the centre of behaviourism. Very often this included animal behaviour, as a kind of scaled-down or simplified model from which human behaviour could be extrapolated. Behaviourism has often been criticised for its 'cold' or 'inhuman' approach, but paradoxically it is perhaps this tradition which offers a more optimistic view of human potentialities and personal change than either psychoanalysis or trait theory. Behaviourism gave us learning theory, and the principles of operant and classical conditioning. 'Conditioning' is a term which needs little explanation nowadays, as it has become embedded in everyday language (although it has often been given meanings not intended by the originators of the concept). The essential and facilitating feature of learning theory is 'that which has been learned can be unlearned'. Phobias could now be seen not as the symbolic expression of an unconscious fear, rooted deep in one's early life, but as anxiety which had become attached, or 'conditioned', to an incidental object at the time of some frightening experience. The phobia could be eradicated by a learning programme in which the person is 'desensitised' to the object, for example by repeatedly pairing the feared object with pleasant (or at least non-fear-inducing) experiences. So behaviourism has at least this much in common with PCP – the belief in the essential changeability (the ability to change) of human beings.

However, there is another fundamental aspect of this approach which contrasts with PCP: whilst it does not see the psychology of human beings as essentially constrained by their biology, it does see them as moulded or determined by environmental events. The behaviourists were interested not in what makes people different from one another (as were the trait theorists) but in identifying universal psychological laws. They felt that in a fundamental way people could be seen as functionally equivalent. They believed it was possible to predict a person's behaviour from a knowledge of the events to which they had been exposed, and that such predictions were valid for any individual. Within a behaviouristic model, it would be appropriate to ask whether being exposed to violence on television increases violent behaviour in people–the problem is that the answer to this question is 'sometimes it does and sometimes it doesn't'. But the fact that people don't all react to the same event in the same way does not prise us away from a widely held assumption that runs through both behaviourism and our common-sense view of the world, and this can be described as 'mechanism' (pertaining to machines). Just as the operation of machines can be thought of as a series of events, each set in motion by the one before and causing the next one (sewing machines, car engines and computers all operate in this way), we think of psychological events as being caused in similar fashion, either by our psychological make-up (trait theory), or by our experiences (psychoanalysis and behaviourism). The 'human machine' thus conceptualised may be extraordinarily complex, but it *is* a machine nonetheless. Within this framework the faults in the human machine are understood in terms of the treatment it has had, or faulty constituent parts, or the unsuitable conditions under which we are expecting it to function. Combinations of forces from within (motives and drives), forces from without (reinforcement contingencies, stimulus–response bonds) and flawed biological material (such as being an extraverted neurotic) are called upon as explanations of the human puzzle. It is understandable that we think of people in such terms, because we live in times where this mechanistic thinking has been very successful in the world of engineering and the natural sciences. If a bridge collapses, we look for causes in terms of its components or forces acting upon it. Perhaps we would accept a combination of causes – wear and tear on cheap materials led to stresses and strains that resulted in the disaster. It's like saying 'well, his neurotic character wasn't suited to such a high-pressure job, that's why he had the breakdown'. Notice that even the language of 'breakdown' and 'stress and strain' are borrowed from the world of the machine. And if we cannot find causes in the environment or characteristic traits, we can always use the explain-all of unconscious motives. Since no one, least of all the sufferer, can examine these, they provide a safe residue of causes for the psychologist.

So we can see that in this respect PCP contrasts sharply with all three models discussed so far. Kelly does not propose that internal states or external events cause our behaviour, thoughts or feelings in this way; it is for this reason that you will not find any reference in PCP to such well-known psychological concepts as 'drive' and 'motivation', ideas which invite us to see people as pushed or pulled by forces they cannot resist. These concepts lead us to imagine that human beings are inert lumps of matter until they are catapulted into action by the relevant drive or need. Kelly saw human beings as in a constant state of psychological motion, perpetually in the process of construing and acting upon their world. Kelly's view of the person can thus be characterised as dynamic rather than static.

Psychoanalysis, behaviourism and trait theory, then, each grew out of particular theoretical and practical climates, and have all enjoyed (and are still to some extent enjoying) a period of enthusiasm and interest. But modern-day psychology has again shifted its focus, away from the 'unconscious' and 'personality' towards theories of mental processing. Psychologists today are more likely to have an interest in information processing, memory or problem solving than in why John Smith suffers extreme anxiety at the thought of leaving the house alone. To some extent, the machine-like notion of the person has been superseded by the question 'to what extent is the brain like a computer?'. This is an oversimplified statement of what cognitive psychology is about, but serves to show up an important difference between much of present-day psychology and PCP. The former is largely about processes, PCP is about whole people. This is why we refer to it as personal construct *psychology* rather than personal construct *theory*. PCP is a complete, internally coherent theory of the person, rather than a theory about any one particular aspect of human functioning. This is why PCP is somewhat misplaced in the 'Personality' section of psychology textbooks.

The psychological models briefly described above are, then, alternative constructions of human beings. Even the idea of personality can be seen to be yet another construction; it is one way of explaining why people differ in their thoughts, feelings and behaviour. Like any classification system, it is just one way of organising what we see to make some sense of it. All classifications are constructions, attempts to make sense of our experience. The question is whether a particular classification makes sense and allows us to do something with it. Psychology itself has only recently (during the past hundred years) been thought of as a (relatively) coherent body of knowledge. For the study of individual behaviour (psychology) to be distinguished from the study of society (sociology) required a conceptualisation that is by no means self-evident, and has no place in Islamic or Taoist societies.

Note that Kelly did not say that it is wrong or inaccurate to think about people in the ways we have described – there are endless alternative constructions we could employ, and many other personality theories have been developed. The question is: where have they got us? And if we are looking for ways of understanding and helping people, Kelly claims the answer is 'not far enough'.

'Personality', then, from Kelly's perspective, is defined in terms of the individual's theories, the way they see the world, their pattern of construction. And PCP is, of course, just another construction – it has no more right to the label of 'truth' than any other. But we believe that it often has more usefulness.

Choice, Change and Reconstruction

We have now introduced issues which are central to the rest of the book, and are elaborated on in Parts I and II. Parts III and IV revolve around a third important issue – that of choice and its role in personal change.

The models of humankind we have outlined so far all carry with them implications for personal change. Whether, and to what extent, personal change is a possibility depends on what perspective, which model of the person you adopt. And each in its turn has implications for *how* such change is attainable.

Many of the problems we shall focus on in the later sections will be only too familiar, and have been deliberately chosen as examples of the commonly experienced desire to change one's life (How can I stop myself from worrying?/smoking?/eating chocolate?). But it must be stressed that this is not a self-help book. We are not recommending a recipe-type approach to solving personal problems. What we are offering is a reconstruction of such problems into a Kellian framework which, we believe, offers a better chance of getting a helpful answer. Kelly said that the main purpose of his theory was to help people to reconstrue their past, so that they were no longer the victims of it. It seeks to help people start afresh – there are to be no concessions to genetics, biologically based temperaments or crippling childhoods. Gargantuan task though this may be, we should act as though it were possible.

It follows that we cannot blame our past for our current failures or difficulties. So does this mean that we only have ourselves to blame for getting into a mess? On the surface of it, it could look as though PCP is simply a reworking of the Victorian ethic, which blamed the poor, and their supposed laziness, for their plight. But this is most definitely not what PCP is suggesting. The question 'who is to blame, me or my past?' is a bad question, which limits the possible answers to two unhelpful alternatives. The construct 'blame self versus blame others' is a good example of how we can become prisoners of our own construing. When people want help to change, they usually cannot use good advice. What is needed is a mixture of reconstruing (the asking of new questions) and action. Kelly offers a radical alternative which frees the notions of responsibility and human agency from the confines of blame, and he does this by showing how an individual's construction of their world is central to the choices they believe to be available to them.

In Part V we look at some of the methods and techniques that have emerged from PCP as ways of facilitating personal change. The aim is to show how these methods bear the hallmark of Kellian theory, and when it may be appropriate to use them.

In the essays that follow, we try to dissect what we see as commonly asked bad questions. In so doing we shall attempt to amplify the Kellian principles we have outlined in this chapter. We hope PCP will come to life in the context of examples, case studies and common dilemmas.

Our aim throughout this book is to provide the reader with the spirit rather than the letter of the theory. At the end of the book is a list of suggested further reading for those who would like to know more about PCP.

Part I
Constructive Alternativism

In this first section, we explore a very Kellian proposition – that of constructive alternativism. It is from this basic tenet that all PCP flows. This fundamental proposition states that events, people, relationships, situations – in fact all the 'things' we have to deal with in our daily lives – do not come bearing labels, ready to slip into convenient, ready-made categories. It is we who construct the categories (such as 'homosexual', 'friend', 'table', 'animal' or 'vegetable') and it is we who impose upon events our own framework (or construction) of categories and dimensions, so that what we perceive around us appears to have order and pattern. The problem is that we can get so used to a particular system of categories and dimensions in the way we approach the world that we end up feeling that what we have are facts rather than one perspective among an infinite number of possible alternative perspectives or constructions.

In Chapter 2 we explore the nature of constructive alternativism and the implications it has not only in our day-to-day lives, but also for how we approach the relationship between facts and theories in any science from psychology to physics.

The next two chapters take as their examples the nature of human relationships. The aim here is to show how, as a culture, we are wedded to particularly rigid constructions of emotional and sexual life, tending to see them as facts rather than as (sometimes very ill-fitting) constructions on our experience. Metaphors for sexuality are explored which do not paint us into the same corner that the idea of 'drive' tends to do.

In the final chapter of this section we examine the nature of a very common construction – that of reason versus emotion, and the psychological costs inherent in it. The aim is to show that if we abandon this construction of human functioning and adopt a more 'wholistic' view, human behaviour begins to look less irrational and more logical (or 'psychological', as Kelly would have preferred).

11

A further theme running through this section is that of 'anticipation'. By this, Kelly meant the way the construct system a person is using sets them to approach the world in one frame of mind rather than another, a state of affairs that subtly moulds their behaviour, and in turn that of the other people around them.

Chapter 2
Is That a Fact?

On the face of it, this hardly sounds like a psychological question at all. It sounds more like, well, a question of fact! Some may regard the question as a philosophical issue, but in the main we tend to assume that we can settle the issue of whether or not something is a fact by an appeal to the evidence and the use of reason. A fact is something which is true for all time, across all situations, surely? Is it not a fact that I am writing with a fountain pen and am a psychologist? To answer this we enter into a process of measuring up this statement against some objective truth, and we answer either 'true' or 'false '. So why is this a psychological issue?

Psychology is concerned with (among other things) human conduct and experience. It seeks to understand why people think, feel and act the way they do. But we must remember that psychology itself is a recent invention. Nowadays we readily discriminate between psychologists, doctors, charlatans, astrologers and philosophers. But such distinctions would not have made sense to anyone living even a century ago. The 'fact' that 'I am a psychologist' could have no meaning for people living then. So already this 'fact' begins to look a bit shaky, or at least on less firm ground than statements such as 'This is a chair' or 'I was born in Manchester'. Perhaps psychologists do not exist in any real sense at all!

The point we are making here is that concepts such as 'fact', 'logic' and psychology are convenient tools which human beings have themselves manufactured, and which they use to help them think about the world. Objects, concepts, events and so on – in fact all the things which make up our conscious day-to-day lives – none of these comes bearing God-given labels. Labels and categories such as 'philosopher' or 'chair' are the result of human psychological activity. We tend to think of such labels and categories as having some intrinsic identity or 'factness' only because they have preceded us as individuals and we personally did not invent them. We shall see that what is considered a fact or a truth varies enormously from one time to another in history, from one place to another, and even from one individual to another. And this is why 'Is that a fact?' is a psychological issue. Once we accept the position that things and events do not have fixed, irrevocable meanings and that there is potentially infinite variety in the alternative meanings or constructions which may be attached to them (Kelly called this 'constructive alternativism'), we can begin to appreciate why it is that people think, feel and act differently from one another. We also have gained a starting point for trying to understand the thoughts, feelings and actions of any particular individual.

Let us take as a simple example the concept of a holiday. If we try to answer the question 'What is a holiday?', we shall soon find that it is extraordinarily difficult to arrive at a definition. Are holidays relaxing or tiring? Enjoyable or stressful? We cannot arrive at a factual, unambiguous answer because they are all (and more) of these things to different people. Once we accept that holidays may be construed as relaxing for one person but stressful for another, we can begin to understand what is at issue for them as their annual fortnight in the sun approaches. We have to understand the underlying meanings or constructs attached to holidays for a person, that is, the way they construe holidays.

We have used two terms in this chapter which are often confused – *concept* and *construct*. Before we go any further, it will be helpful to discriminate between them and explain what is meant by each. Beginners in PCP often think that the two terms are synonymous, and it is important to understand the difference at the outset. *Concept* is a term that comes from logic. A concept is a kind of category into which things are (metaphorically) put, on the basis of some common factor or classification system. 'Vegetable', 'furniture', 'science' and 'psychology' are concepts, and we use them in our day-to-day lives. We 'have' concepts in the sense that they are pigeon holes which we carry around with us in our heads, forming part of the framework for our mental processes. We do not 'have' constructs in the same way: we have constructs in the same way that we have questions and it makes more sense to talk about construing as something we *do*. Construing is a process, it is one of the things we do. Construing is how we use concepts. We use a category system of concepts to help us make sense of the world and to give us guidance in how to act in our everyday lives. So if we say 'Oh, she's a psychologist!', we have used the concept 'psychologist' in a particular and probably idiosyncratic way: perhaps we have seen two people talk and were wondering which was the psychologist and which was the patient; or perhaps, watching the same conversation, we are puzzled by the intimate nature of the content, and the fact that the person we are watching is a psychologist and not an acquaintance or a lawyer or a salesperson helps us to get our bearings and understand what is going on. In each case, we are 'construing' the social event that we are watching and asking a question – psychologist or patient? psychologist or acquaintance?, etc. In each case it is a question that has an either/or format. Construing has to have this dichotomous form. The meaning that emerges for us from our questioning does so through this process of contrast and, discrimination. Thus 'psychologist' and 'patient' are concepts, but 'psychologist or patient?' and 'psychologist or lawyer?' are constructs, questions we pose ourselves in order to make sense of our experience. We shall look more closely at the nature of constructs and construing in later chapters.

So far we have introduced the notion of constructive alternativism, indicated how it has important implications for psychology, and explained the difference between concepts and constructs. Let us now go on to explore further assumptions which are implicit in the question 'Is that a fact?'.

Just as when we ask the question 'Is she a psychologist?' we are implicitly also asking '...or a lawyer/acquaintance, etc.', the question 'Is that a fact?' holds a possible alternative answer – '...or a fiction?', '...or a rumour?.' '...or a theory?' So we can point out, as it were in passing, that asking the question 'Is that a fact?' is itself the manifestation of construing. The construct we are using may be 'fact versus fiction' or 'fact versus theory', but whichever it is we can begin to see that constructs, unlike concepts, always have an opposite end to them, that is they are bipolar. It would make no sense to ask what is the logical opposite of the concept 'psychologist': it could only be 'not a psychologist'.

This means that when we ask 'Is that a fact?' we are always (and often implicitly or non-consciously) contrasting 'facts' with something else. Usually the 'fact' end of the construct has the feeling of something indisputable, of definite shape, not affected by whimsy or observation. The contrast is usually. thought of as softer than hard fact – associated perhaps with theory, imagination, fantasy or opinion. Hard facts are thought of as the province of science, a no-nonsense, masculine domain where we can call a spade a spade, with no room for sentiment or involvement. Indeed, these latter characterise the feminine contrast pole of the arts, where passion has its place (albeit an inferior one) in our present high-tech society. But these constellations of meaning say more about our construing than about the truths that we are trying to come to grips with. Constructs like masculine–feminine, rational–emotional and art–science are the responsibility of people, the construers, and do not represent real qualities inherent in events themselves. (We use the term 'event' to describe any object of a construal or question, since it seems the best the English language can come up with.) The construer uses dimensions and terms of reference that are available and that they are familiar with in order to help get their bearings.

The day of the 'hard fact' as bankable currency, a nugget of truth in a world of muddy theory is, however, long since past. It was born in the nineteenth century, the era of Newtonian physics and the youthful flush of science. Contemporary physics is highly theoretical and facts seem thin on the ground. No one, for example, tells us what an electron is, or what it would look like. 'For some purposes it is construed as though it were a particle and for others a wave. It can be treated as though it were either. This ambiguity is tolerated and is not the basis of a serious dispute. It is accepted that electrons exist, but the search for the 'fact' of what an electron really is no longer occupies scientists. The lack of such facts has not prevented theorising that has led to the development of atomic power. What then is the nature of the relationship between theory and facts? Surely there are truths, facts, that exist and theories have to account for them? You cannot have whimsical theories that fly in the face of the facts? Actually, the relationship is very much a chicken-and-egg one. Certainly theories have to take account of available evidence, but the theories also decide what *counts* as evidence. Carr (1961) takes as an example of a historical fact Caesar's crossing of the Rubicon. He points out that countless millions have also crossed the Rubicon and yet these 'facts' have gone unrecorded. Caesar also crossed many other rivers and no one has paid heed. The crossing of the Rubicon is seen as a fact because of its significance in signalling Caesar's rebellion against the Roman republic. History is, by definition, written in retrospect. It highlights facts that fit its narrative and ignores those that do not. History is not a simple chronicle of facts; it is a theory, a story that makes sense of the past, and in so doing raises certain facts to prominence. At the beginning of this chapter I listed two facts about myself: psychologist writing with a fountain pen. Of the millions of facts I could have selected why pick these two? There are more important facts, more central to me, that I could have focused on, but these two are not trivial. They are relevant to my theory about myself, my self-construing, particularly in the context of what I am now doing, i.e. writing a chapter.

As theories change, frameworks shift (or history is rewritten?), different facts come into focus and we notice systematic elements that had formerly appeared random. So any fact or truth does not stand on its own. It has significance only within a particular theory. Likewise any theory, fantasy or speculation relies on facts to support it. It is very like the relationship between the awesome and beautiful cathedral and its component stone: no stone, no building. But without the building, the stone would be insignificant rubble, or invisible, buried beneath the earth. The stone is sought, mined and fashioned with a purpose in mind.

This way of looking at the relationship between fact and theory is also useful when it comes to understanding people. In fact Kelly suggested that we look at people 'as if' they were scientists, engaged in a constant process of putting their theories to the test, the facts supporting or discrediting the theories, but at the same time the theories spotlighting some facts rather than others. When faced with people's theories, or the facts they present us with, we must never lose sight of this dialectic process. Any fact can look convincing, given the context of a good argument. The wildest conspiracy theory about international communism/capitalism/Zionism can seem plausible until we hear an advocate for an alternative construction. If we now bring together the two ideas of 'person-as-scientist' and constructive alternativism, we can see that the terms 'theory' and 'construct' are not very far apart. When Kelly suggested that we view people as if they were scientists, he meant that their conduct, thoughts and feelings are intimately bound up with the theories they are currently holding, the questions (constructs) with which they approach the world.

Let us now set these ideas in the context of an illustrative example.

> Caroline sought help from a psychotherapist, insisting that wherever she went people looked at her in a disapproving, faintly shocked way. She was convinced that they thought she looked rather odd, perhaps slightly 'butch' and she certainly had no shortage of evidence for her theory. She could become angry, anxious and defiant as she read onlookers' thinly veiled hostility in their faces, and gradually she was becoming more of a recluse. As in any experiment, validatory evidence led to the strengthening of a theory that was beginning to dominate her life. The 'facts' were difficult to establish since the therapist could not be a fly on the wall at all Caroline's encounters, but it was unlikely that this persecutory theory was totally crazy. After all, sometimes people do look oddly at you, although this does not register unless your radar is specifically tuned in to it.

For the facts to lodge, a certain perceptual set is necessary. When you begin to anticipate disapproval it is invariably betrayed in posture, deed and word. A hunted look, a furtive glance, a jerky movement certainly attract attention, which of course fulfils the prophesy. Convincing someone that they are wrong in a case like this simply by questioning the facts is virtually impossible. Mahoney (1974) cites the case of a schizophrenic patient who insisted that he was dead. 'Do dead people bleed?' asked the exasperated psychiatrist. 'No', replied the patient, whereupon the doctor pricked the patient's finger and produced a drop of blood. 'Oh God, the dead *do* bleed!' was the response.

Like some professional scientists, people often manipulate the data in a way that fits their theories. The Kellian proposition is that even a theory with painful outcomes is better than no theory at all (we shall come back to this in later chapters). Nothing is worse than having the ground shift beneath your feet. In an attempt to prevent such a psychological earthquake, people 'cook the books', deceive themselves, and this is frequently interpreted as hostility by others who are hurt, shunned or disregarded in the process. As facts do not have any importance outside their theoretical context, they cannot be disputed without challenging the theories of which they are an integral part. So the task for Caroline's therapist was not to try to discount the evidence around which Caroline had built her theory, but to gain an understanding of the construing which underlay it, and to guide her towards an alternative way of construing herself and others which did not land her with a self-damaging theory.

To call something a fact is usually to claim for it an independent status – to claim that meaning belongs to it and is not conferred upon it. In our efforts to apprehend truths we invent theories, generate meaning, create facts. We cannot easily separate the things we perceive from the way we perceive them – the event from the construction of it. This smell is disgusting, that sight terrifying, and that music relaxing. But these qualities do not reside in the phenomena, only in our experience of them. It does not, of course, feel to us as though these meanings are inferred. It feels as though they are properties of the perceived events. We do not see something and then decide it is terrifying. We see it as terrifying. The construction is in the perception, part of the definition of the fact.

This is not to deny that truth exists, independent of observers. An electron is not a figment of the imagination. Its nature, however, is a mystery along with infinity and a whole host of things about people. We must not jump to conclusions, imagining that we have the patent on the truth. Today's facts have a notorious habit of turning into tomorrow's jokes, though the deeds carried out in their name often render them black humour. Facts about people are even more elusive than facts about the natural world. Stefan (1977) suggests that we can think of truths as falling roughly into three categories:

1. those that remain true despite the telling of them, e.g. 'there is a desk in the corner';
2. those that become true because of their telling, e.g. labelling people as 'difficult' leads to treating them as such and sets in motion a self-fulfilling prophesy;
3. those that become less true because of their telling, e.g. telling someone your prediction of their actions can lead to their doing exactly the opposite.

Although truths of types 2 and 3 abound in the social sciences, the problem is that we tend to think that all truths are of type 1.

In the next two chapters, we continue to look at constructive alternativism and consider its implications for personal relationships and sexuality.

Chapter 3
Are You Friends or Lovers?

This is a question which is not only a silent query hanging over many of our relationships, but is also frequently given verbal expression. It represents an issue that appears personally and culturally important, and the question is the concrete manifestation of this issue.

In our Western society, love is big business. It is the subject of popular music, fiction, poetry and everyday talk. It is there on the television screen, and in the cinema. It is the energy behind life, death, happiness and tragedy.

Given our preoccupation with the role of love in our lives, it seems odd that psychologists have paid it little attention. How could such a burning issue escape the notice of the very people whose aim it is to understand human experience and behaviour?

For one reason, psychologists have for a long time traditionally fought shy of things that could not be observed and measured. Students of psychology who expected to learn something personally relevant in the psychological study of 'emotion' often found themselves measuring only levels of adrenaline and noradrenaline in the laboratory white rat.

Another reason why psychologists have steered around the issue is because, in a rather subtle way, it is taboo. This sounds nonsense in the face of the ever-present love theme in the media, but a taboo on a subject does not necessarily mean that people don't *mention* it. Death is a good example. Death is always in the news. It happens all the time. People even joke about it. But this very humour shows that there is a restricted number of ways of publicly talking about death. Humour is often a vehicle for 'saying' the most disturbing things, without really *talking* about them. It is a device, a code, used between people to acknowledge the most threatening issues without having to confront and engage them.

In many ways, love is in the same boat. Yes, we talk about love all the time; but aside from the culturally sanctioned formulae (boy meets girl, they fall in love and live happily ever after) against which all other scenarios appear deviant or wrong, we don't openly give voice to the ways in which love is problematic for us - for the person who feels that they hate their mother or resent their child, or feels confused about their sexuality, the taboo is still an effective silencer.

What all this amounts to is that societally and culturally we talk as if we had love sewn up. We can even talk knowledgeably about different kinds of love (mother love, romantic love, brotherly love, etc). But privately we stare at the grey areas of our own feelings and relationships and wonder where it all fits. For some people this may never come to more than occasional vague unease, for example when a married man feels attracted to someone other than his wife. For others, such as as gay people, the issue is ever present in their lives and represents a conflict (private behaviour and experience versus public acceptability) which struggles for resolution.

The question in the title of this chapter represents one such source of unease, one way in which we privately and publicly acknowledge the way in which we sometimes don't have love sewn up in a nice neat parcel. We shall show how PCP can shed light on how we came to be in this position in the first place, and how it can help us out of the corner into which we have painted ourselves.

In Chapter 2, we saw that PCP proposes that it is part of the fundamental nature of human beings to make sense of our experience by looking for common themes, by adopting dimensions which roughly sort our experiences into meaningful categories, which Kelly called constructs. We explore more fully the role of constructs in how we think about ourselves and others in later chapters, where we will meet examples such as 'practical versus creative' and 'peaceful versus aggressive'. Constructs are always dimensions which make sense to the individual, and are not necessarily combinations of what would generally be judged to be logical opposites. ('Practical', in this sense, would have 'impractical' as its logical opposite. In the previous chapter, we noted that the idea of 'facts' implied an opposite, which could be, for example, 'fiction' or 'theory'.)

However, given the social nature of human life, it would be surprising indeed if each and every construct used by individuals were unique. The use of language demands that, in order to communicate meaningfully, we need access to a set of mutually agreed concepts and ideas. When I talk to you about the holiday I spent last summer, we both need roughly to agree on what a holiday is. With a concept like 'holiday', as we have already seen, there is a fairly wide range of implied individual difference; for one person it may mean two weeks lying in the sun on a foreign beach, for another it may mean an expedition to the top of Ben Nevis. But for other concepts the range of possibly included experiences is much narrower. When I say I went for a job interview, the possible range of experiences and behaviours this could include is quite restricted and subject to more rules (or 'norms') which govern these behaviours and experiences.

We could do this exercise with just about any concept or idea in our language. What would emerge is that, for any given idea or concept, people generally can agree upon roughly what it can describe and what it can't. There will, of course, be disagreements: some would argue that the job of lecturer does not constitute 'real work', and we might argue that housework also ought to be incorporated within the idea of 'real work'.

The point is that some of the categories and dimensions we use to fit our experience in order to make sense of it are not idiosyncratic: they are culturally available, mutually agreed upon and, furthermore, are indispensible if we are to communicate meaningfully with other people.

When it comes to love, these culturally available categories and dimensions are of the 'job-interview' rather than the 'holiday' type. The rules governing what constitutes a friend, a lover, or a mother are really quite strict. What we really mean by romantic love, platonic love or mother love is similarly well defined, and is governed by a particularly strict set of rules, or norms - moral rules, i.e. there is an especially forceful feeling of 'should' and 'ought' attached to our thinking about the feelings and behaviour that go into these categories. What *should* a mother do? What *ought* a friend *not* do? We feel keenly the implied (or actual) censure of society when these rules are broken.

So far this sounds like common sense. We have been describing what is known or implicitly realised by everyone who shares a society and a culture. But what we fail to remind ourselves of, like the individual whose system of constructs has become more of a hindrance than help to them, is that these are dimensions which we have ourselves placed upon our experience. Categories such as 'mother love', 'gay' or even 'holidays' do not exist independently of human thought (unless one believes that they are God given, in which case the problem takes on a very different nature). Events and experiences do not come bearing, labels. We (either as individuals or as a society or culture) give them a name in order to make some sense of it all. This organising feature of human nature is fundamentally necessary, but it also brings pitfalls. We come to see the pattern we have imposed as the only possible one rather than one perspective among many. Thus 'mother love', 'romantic love', 'gay love' and 'platonic love' appear to us as basic facts of life rather than as possible (and sometimes not very efficient) ways of dividing up our emotional experiences.

Because of the self-evident feel of these categories, and because the rules governing this area of our lives are so strong, it is not surprising that questions such as 'Is she your friend or your lover?', and 'Am I straight or gay' (bipolar constructs) loom large in our introspection. Let us look at a case study as an example of how such a question became problematic for two people.

Mick was in his thirties, and had been married to Helen for ten years. Their three children were all now at school, and life at home was gradually losing the somewhat chaotic nature it had assumed when the children were small. Both his and Helen's jobs were going well, and he considered that, at least compared with many men he knew, he was happy in his marriage. Like most couples, Mick and Helen found that sometimes their relationship could not fulfil all of their individual needs. Helen felt that, in common with many other men, Mick found it difficult to be demonstrably emotionally supportive when she was having a particularly worrying time, although she never doubted that he cared deeply about her and their family. Fortunately, she had a close girlfriend who was always ready to listen and provide the extra support she needed. Mick felt that he and Helen were ideally suited in many ways, but one thing he had never really been able to share with her was his love of poetry. Since being a teenager, he had felt a keen attraction for this mode of writing, and had even set down a few verses of his own. Helen was enthusiastic on his behalf when he had these creative moments, but her interest was, he felt, born of her feelings for him rather than of a liking for the subject matter. In the early years of their marriage, when all their energies were focused on caring for their young family and getting established in their careers, there simply hadn't seemed to be time to think about poetry. But now Mick was beginning to feel the urge to resume his old interest, and decided to join a local poetry-reading circle. The group consisted of eight or so men and women of various ages who met once a fortnight to read and discuss poetry.

One of the other members was a woman called Jane, who was also married and had a young daughter. Mick and Jane immediately 'hit it off' together. They quickly found that they felt drawn to the same poets and were 'on the same wavelength' when they discussed the thoughts and feelings that their reading had evoked.

Within a relatively short time, Mick found that Jane had come to have a place in his life which was very important to him. Together they explored, discussed and charted what was for them new intellectual and emotional ground, and their relationship became very close. They were confidantes, mentors, friends, and there was a strong bond of affection between them.

Their relationship began to excite comment from those who observed them together, and it became obvious that an affair was rumoured. It was at this point that the relationship began to pose awkward questions for Mick and Jane. Were they friends or lovers? While each could honestly say that they had no wish for an affair, the term 'friend' seemed totally inadequate to describe their relationship. They *were* friends, and yet they shared as much affection as many married couples they knew. They were not lovers, and yet there was an emotional attachment between them, the nature of which they felt would not have been the same between two men or two women – the fact that Mick was a man and Jane a woman was not irrelevant to the relationship. In the face of the implied question mark over the nature of their relationship, Mick and Jane soon began to doubt their own feelings. Perhaps they really *were* looking for an affair and not admitting it to themselves. Certainly it would be easy to take the step which would lead them down that road...

We shall leave their story open-ended and discuss what has happened, and could happen, in the light of PCP.

Faced with the culturally available and mutually exclusive categories of 'friend' and 'lover', Mick and Jane had to squeeze their relationship into the one thing they felt offered best fit. On the rule that 'if it isn't one of these, it must be one of those', it seemed to them that 'friends' was such a poor description of them that perhaps they really were 'lovers'. 'Friend versus lover' is a dimension (a construct) along which in our culture we typically evaluate relationships, and one where it is considered impossible to occupy the middle ground, You have to choose which end of the construct your relationship occupies.

The next important point to make is that the very existence of these dimensions exerts a terrific pull on people's behaviour and experience. It is rather like the labelling phenomenon described by sociologists – for example, if you call someone a delinquent, pretty soon they begin to behave like one, The subtle way in which our expectations of people gently mould their behaviour and experience is usually not felt at a conscious level. In a similar way to the delinquency example, if Mick and Jane and the people around them come to see their relationship as rather more like 'lovers' than 'friends', the general tone of their interactions and conversations will find itself channelled in this direction. Kelly referred to the way our constructs predispose us emotionally and cognitively to experience and behave in some ways rather than others as 'anticipation'.

Thus, the anticipations attached to the construct 'friend versus lover' exert their own subtle pressures. So not only do rigidly applied dimensions such as these give rise to anxiety for those who can't find a good fit, the attempt to impose a badly fitting dimension upon one's experience can artificially trigger an unnecessary move towards one end of the dimension. The problem is even clearer with the issue of homosexuality, which is explored more fully in the next chapter. It is easy to understand how a young person, experiencing for the first time the many-faced creature of his or her own sexuality, may attempt to locate themselves on the culturally available dimension of gay/straight and ask 'Am I one of these or one of those?'. It is often an inappropriate question, but the pressure to answer it can have far-reaching consequences .

Concepts such as 'anticipation' and 'labelling' account for how people feel that they have drifted into a way of life they never intended or wanted. It can have a 'fated' feel about it. This is perhaps the most insidious aspect of the phenomenon, because it can feel as though people have relatively little choice or control in how their lives turn out – 'I never wanted an affair – it just happened and I couldn't do anything about it'. The couple in our case study, at the point where we left them, felt keenly that they *could* choose to go down the path that led to an affair. Equally, they *could* choose to alter their relationship in such a way as to fit it more easily into the 'friends' end of the dimension. There was no over-arching, definitive feature of their relationship which made the decision a foregone conclusion. Kelly insists that we always choose (within the limits of practical constraints) the direction of our lives – but we are not always conscious of having done so, hence the 'destined' feel of 'becoming a homosexual' or 'drifting into an affair'. The big problem for Mick and Jane, should they choose to continue to tread the line between 'friend' and 'lover', or even to abandon this construct altogether as an appropriate question to ask of their relationship (in Kellian terms, their relationship would be out of the range of convenience of the construct 'friend versus lover'), is that they will also have abandoned their society's common language for talking about relationships, and are putting nothing in its place. This presents surprisingly commonplace problems that at first glance appear trivial. For example, how do you refer to a person one lives with but is not married to? Cohabitee? Live-in lover? Common-law spouse? These are easy enough to use when filling in a government form, but are they any good for everyday conversation? The relationships they attempt to describe do not have the shared sets of meanings, norms and values attached to 'husband' and 'wife'. The problem is even more complex for gay relationships.

The value of a PCP approach to this problem is in the principle of constructive alternativism. This means that there are an infinite number of possible ways of construing our experience, and some constructions will be more useful than others in making sense of what we perceive, feel and think. We tend to get rather attached to some constructions, such as 'friend–lover', so that it comes to seem to us that this is the only possible way of looking at things. Once we realise that this is the case, the anxiety and confusion we feel when our experience doesn't fit becomes understandable, and we can begin to experiment with more useful constructs which offer us a way of making sense of our relationships without leading us down paths we do not wish to travel. This does not mean that we can simply think away the problems entailed in constructs such as 'friend versus lover'. But to the extent that the way we construe our relationships is manifested in the way we live those relationships, a reconstruction along dimensions that do not look like 'friend–lover' is an important starting point in the slow process of social change. In the next chapter, we offer such a reconstruction of the question 'Am I gay?'.

Chapter 4
Am I Gay?

This chapter continues our examination of constructive alternativism, in the context of sexuality and sexual identity. One of the points we made in Chapter 3 is that culturally available constructs like 'friend-lover' exert an enormous pull upon the form our relationships take and our experience of them, giving rise to problems in how we represent our relationships to ourselves. We argued that such constructs are not always helpful in making sense of our emotional experiences and that a reconstruction along different dimensions would be fruitful.

Gay sexuality is another case where a culturally available construct carrying great moral weight (homosexual versus heterosexual) often creates more problems for us than it solves. In this chapter we expose the dimension 'heterosexual-homosexual' as a culturally agreed upon construct similar, in this sense, to 'friend-lover'. But a second important point that we wish to make is to do with the nature of identity. We want to suggest that there is a very important difference between practising (or fantasising about) a gay act and being gay, in the same way as there is a difference between acting neurotically and being a neurotic, or between smoking a lot and being a nicotine addict. Neuroticism and addiction are issues that we shall return to in later chapters.

Foucault (1981) and Weeks (1986) show us that homosexuals, as a class of people having a particular sexual identity or orientation, are a relatively recent invention. They are not denying that gay acts are as old as recorded history. Gay relationships in ancient Greece were an integral feature of civilised life. A mature man 'adopted' a youth, for whom he took the role of mentor and guide, and homosexual practices were seen as a normal and proper part of such a relationship; in fact they were part of the mechanisms whereby mature men demonstrated their masculinity. The social norms attached to gay acts meant that a mature man must adopt an active or dominant sexual role, and this was possible only with women (who were seen as inferior) and youths (who had not yet attained full manhood). Gay acts between adult men were seen as demeaning to the one who adopted the passive role.

The idea of gay practices as a feature of masculinity seems ludicrous in the context of our present-day attitudes towards sexuality, and the frankness with which such practices were acknowledged and accepted shocks many today. In the Victorian era, which had so much invested in the denial and repression of sexuality, the facts of sexual history could be dealt with only by inventing the notion that it was just such sexual licence that must have led to the downfall of the ancient empires.

The point that we are trying to make is that gay practices have always been commonplace, but it is only in relatively recent historical times that we have begun to think of *people* as gay (as opposed to straight); the construct 'heterosexual–homosexual' was simply not in use. Nowadays when we call someone a gay, a statement is being made which goes beyond a description of his or her sexual practices. It implies that they have a sexual orientation which can be seen as being part of their personality, the kind of person they are. It goes beyond this too, because along with 'gay' comes a whole host of other characteristics which we imagine must also belong to a person with this identity. For example, gay men are often thought of as effeminate, rather like our outdated stereotype of women, so they are imagined to be more sensitive, artistic and delicate than other men. The way they speak and walk is also similarly caricatured. In later chapters we shall look at the issue of typologies in personality, that is, the idea that certain personality characteristics 'hang together', giving us different personality types, and we conclude that people are far more likely to see various traits and qualities coalescing into types than is justified by objective evidence. But even if, in some very general way, such types did exist in reality, how bizarre it would be if they hinged on sexual preference! Gore Vidal once asked why we don't expect Bertrand Russell and Lyndon Johnson to be similar characters – after all, they were both heterosexual.

When as a society we feel threatened or puzzled by deviance (by this we mean behaviours which depart from the norm in any given society) we often create identities which revolve around constellations of traits and which we project on to those we consider deviant. The notion of a 'vegetarian' is a nice example of an identity which has only recently evolved. Although vegetarians pose less of a threat and are treated more affectionately than gay people; their case provides a good example. There have always been people who have eaten no meat, and for a variety of reasons – poverty, availability and religion as well as choice. Yet now we think of vegetarianism as associated with a whole set of attitudes and habits. If you think you are immune to social stereotyping, ask yourself these questions. Is a vegetarian more likely:

1. to be politically right wing or left wing?
2. to have gone to university or left school at 16?
3. to read *The Guardian* or *The Sun*?
4. to wear open-toed sandals or smart black shoes?
5. to live in Glasgow or rural Wales?
6. to work in education or commerce?

Then ask yourself what your evidence is for your beliefs. Our bet is that you will realise your prejudices as you go through the list, hopefully with a smile. We tend to carry around an image of ourselves as somehow outside society, and able to distance ourselves from its influences. But this is an illusion–society is not 'out there'; it exists inside each of us in the form of the ideas and assumptions we share. We all constitute society and jointly reproduce its myths. The 'typical' neurotic, alcoholic or homosexual is at best a statistical artefact, and often pure invention. Occasionally we do meet someone who conforms to the theory and, just like scientists who are eager to have their pet theory confirmed, we say 'there you are, I knew it was true!' There are always plenty of people who are nothing like the stereotype. Alexander the Great had a man as a lover, but 'sensitive' and 'gentle' were not words often used to describe him. And it is always worth reminding ourselves that Hitler was a vegetarian.

Not only does the culturally prevalent construct of 'homosexual – heterosexual' mean that we have become locked into seeing people as either one or the other, it invites us to construe them along a whole host of other dimensions too. As we saw in Chapter 3, our construal of others is manifested through the way we anticipate what they will say and do, so that anticipation can encourage or even coerce people into role-slots that are provided for them. In Kellian terms, 'gay' is a pre-emptive label. This means that once identified as gay, you are thought of as nothing but gay. It is the main thing about you, it cancels out other qualities you may have, and prescribes the way you are to be treated. This situation began to emerge when Victorian moralism coincided with the advent of psychiatric diagnosis. Against a social background of sexual hypocrisy and muscular Christianity, nineteenth century doctors began to categorise various types of sexual 'perverts'. Sadists, masochists, fetishists, transvestites and homosexuals came into existence as discrete categories of human sexual identity, and individuals who didn't quite fit the description were more likely to be seen as exceptions that proved the rule than evidence that the classification system itself was a nonsense. But human sexuality is extremely diverse. Our sexuality varies with time, place and circumstance. We may fantasise scenarios that we have no intention of practising, and recognise that some we would not in reality enjoy. We all know our own secrets and nobody else's and tend to be both more puzzled and more ashamed of our sexuality than any other area of our life. Consequently it is very common for people to wonder if there is something wrong with them when they catch themselves enjoying a 'perverted' fantasy.

What we have outlined so far is the nature of homosexuality as it is commonly construed in our present-day society. We have demonstrated some of the evils that arise from such a construction, and have shown that the 'gay–straight' dimension is a relatively recent feature of the way we think about sexuality. Our construction, then, is only one among many possible ways we might construe sexuality. But why has such a construction taken hold of us if it does not reflect some ultimate truth about sexuality? We have said that the blame for thinking in terms of oversimplified categories lies with the nineteenth-century sexologists. But if these ideas were so crazy, why did they take root and flourish? One clue is in the increasing power and prestige of the medical profession. Physicians had acquired the expert status and authority to declare where truth resided in a wide range of human affairs. This status came from a growing faith in 'reductionist' explanations – if we take things apart we shall find out how they work. Tremendous advances in biological knowledge were being made as it became possible to identify smaller and smaller units of matter; the body could be reduced to a knowledge of its constituent parts, which would reveal how the whole thing worked. The success of biological reductionism has led to it being taken as a model for finding out about all sorts of things, not just biology. The language of the biologist has come to be used in explanations of psychology too, so that we tend to think of all human behaviour and experience as ultimately reducible to and explainable by biological events. This is especially true of sexuality, that realm of human experience and behaviour which seems to us especially rooted in the biological. When we construe sexuality as a biological phenomenon, we are led towards some kinds of questions rather than others. We ask what anomalies of body chemistry might account for gay sexuality, or which pheromones are responsible for interpersonal attraction. The problem with biological accounts of sexuality is that they carry with them a feeling of inevitability – it's just the way you're *made*. As a consequence of this, sexual deviance comes to be seen as the result of a mistake in one's chemistry. This brings with it its own problems, which we shall look at more closely in Chapter 14.

It is very hard for us not to feel that we must be talking about biology when we talk about sexuality, but what we are suggesting is that this is only one way of construing sexuality, one perspective among many possible alternatives. The principle of constructive alternativism helps us to distance ourselves and separate event from construction. The prevalence of a biological construction must not blind us to possible alternatives, though a further problem is that the all-pervading nature of reductionist biological constructions has meant that good social/psychological accounts have often not been advanced. However, Plummer (1975; 1995) has provided the foundations of such a view of sexuality, and what follows owes much to his ideas.

The biological construction of sexuality has led to our thinking of it as a drive – like hunger or thirst. It is as though we each have within us a powerful motor, driving us relentlessly onwards. The best we can hope to do is steer it, and indeed we even speak of sexual orientation as if we were talking of some internal direction finder. Perversion is thus seen to occur when this direction finder goes wrong. Instead of following a straight path, our radar gets homed in on some inappropriate target. If our sexuality is a force, a source of energy. It follows that we should have neither too much nor too little: excess leads to lethargic dissipation, even madness and blindness, but the endless jokes about monks in monasteries caution us to beware the celibate whose engine is revving wildly in neutral.

The notion of drive is a nice lesson in the power of metaphor to imprison our thinking and restrict our vision. When we talk metaphorically, we import a whole realm of construction from one context to another. But we can often forget that we began with a metaphor (considering something as if it were something else, just as poets do when they consider lips as roses). We come to mistake event for construction and take it as given that, say, sexuality *is* a driving force, the primary energy of life that determines our character and even our society (as Freud certainly believed). Many feminists would argue that this is primarily a male perspective on sexuality, accounting for essentially male sexual experience.

Plummer proposes an alternative metaphor to 'drive' – that of 'script'. Whereas the notion of drive comes from the world of the machine (i.e. mechanism), script comes from the world of theatre. In drama, there are many different plots and genres, and different scripts await different actors. But this does not mean that our behaviour is totally predetermined. In many dramas, those involved have considerable freedom in how they interpret their roles, or what they read into the script. There is room for 'doing it my way'. But roles and scripts are subordinate, in the play as a whole, to the overall plot; the roles and scripts have some room for manoeuvre, but the plot essentially stays the same. What would it mean, then, to adopt the script as a metaphor for human sexuality, to construe our sexual behaviour and experience as if we were actors in a play rather than libido-driven machines?

If the way the actor interprets the script and stage directions depends on the kind of play he or she is currently in, sexuality must be seen as dependent upon its social context. We can begin to conceive of sexuality as rather more a function of the social life in which it occurs than a determinant of it. Looked at from this perspective, being in the navy, going to prison or attending a public school do not 'bring out' latent gay sexuality in men. But if sexuality is seen as a way of structuring affectionate relationships, and the only people around are of the same sex, it is not surprising that gay sexuality flourishes. What we are saying is that sexuality, like so much of our behaviour and experience, varies according to context. Once we accept the idea that only acts, and not people, can be gay or straight, and if we adopt the 'script' rather than the 'drive' metaphor for sexuality, we can begin to appreciate that sexuality varies according to context, and that potentially infinite variations are possible. We have, in the commonly accepted construal of sexuality, a particularly appealing (though in the end damaging) version of a story, a version we have come to believe in as the only possible way the story can be told. What Kelly reminds us, in the principle of constructive alternativism, is that no construction has the monopoly on truth. The idea of 'perversions' is possible only if we continue to insist that the version of the story we are used to is the right one (simply because we are accustomed to it); and if there are no perversions, only variations, there can be no perverts. We can begin to see that a reconstrual of sexuality has far-reaching implications for how we think about people that are, at the very least, more facilitative than the old 'drive' metaphor. We may even be free to rewrite our 'script' in a way that gives us better options for the future.

Sexual meanings, then, do not reside in objects or practices; meanings are conferred on them by individuals who come to place this or that construction upon their world, and this construction will vary not only between individuals but also between time, place and context. Is a bare breast sexual? Or a piece of black lacy underwear? Or a spanking? Surely it depends on who you are and what the context is. There is no such thing as a sexual act *per se*. Sexual meaning is always conferred upon acts by the people involved in them. Intercourse may have virtually no sexual meaning at all to the couple who feel obliged to go through the ritual for the thousandth time, or the prostitute to whom it is a way of earning a living.

So, from a PCP perspective, 'Am I gay?' is a psychologically meaningless question. A gay wish, fantasy or act does not commit you to an exclusive gay identity; nor does it commit you to a style of life or a particular personality. However, as we saw in the previous chapter, it is a brave person who tries to defy the categories, expectations and anticipations of others. Individual reconstruing is not necessarily echoed throughout the rest of society. But surely there can be no such change without it.

In the next chapter, we see how a great deal of human experience has come to be construed along a single dimension, that of rational versus emotional. We look at the kinds of problem this construction leaves us with, and contrast it with an alternative PCP approach.

Chapter 5
Are You Ruled by Your Head or Your Heart?

Here is a question which presents itself whenever we feel that our reason counsels us to take one course of action, but our feelings seem to be driving us to do something else. Perhaps we are tempted to embark on a love affair, though our reason tells us it would be madness in the light of previous experience. Or perhaps we want to take revenge, though we know it will only perpetuate a vicious circle of violence that we deplore. So what in the end will govern our action, our reason or our emotions?

When we experience such dilemmas, it seems to us that we are like machines, ready to run out of control unless we apply the brake of rationality. This way of thinking owes a great deal to Freud, whose ideas have infiltrated our everyday thought and language to such an extent that we often do not realise that we are adopting a Freudian perspective. It is commonplace to hear people talk about their ego, or to refer to their unconscious wishes when trying to account for some aspect of their behaviour. The idea of animalistic drives and emotions as the driving force of human life, a force which must be constantly held in check in civilised societies, is a Freudian notion that has enjoyed immense popularity. It is so universally accepted that it seems to us the natural way of thinking about human beings.

The key theme in this idea is that we all have a thin veneer of rationality which conceals dark and mysterious forces; the angers and lusts of Mr Hyde held in check by the fragile Dr Jekyll. It is as if we are all really two people, the rational, logical and civilised part of us (the neocortex?) in constant struggle for supremacy over our impulsive emotional, animal part (our 'gut' feelings). This way of thinking is perpetuated and legitimated by introductory psychology texts, which normally carry separate chapters on cognition, emotion and motivation. It is as though these are functions residing in different sorts of hardware in the body; thinking is done with the brain whereas feelings are visceral, originating in our internal organs.

Emotions are thought of as primitive, belonging to an earlier stage of evolution, whereas thought and reason are faculties that have developed along with our higher position in the phylogenetic scale. We like to think of ourselves as rational beings who have triumphed over our environment and our baser animal instincts by the power of our intellect. That this is, however, a theory rather than a fact is clear after only a moment's reflection. A cat does not act out of blind spite and vengeance; indeed the domestic cat often seems like the most rational member of the household, only placing one paw in front of the other if it is absolutely necessary. The vengeful shark in *Jaws* and the lusty King Kong are human projections, allowing humankind to fear and hate 'lower' animals while busily destroying the planet.

It will be apparent by now that what we have in this reason versus emotion dimension is a theory about how human beings function. It is one way of construing human experience, one way of carving up the psychological territory in the attempt to make sense of it. But the principle of constructive alternativism reminds us that this is all it is – a construction, not a description of a real state of affairs. 'Reason versus emotion' is an example of what Kelly called a construct – a dimension or system of categories which people use to order and make sense of their experience. But sometimes, as we shall see throughout this book, our constructs end up being more of a hindrance than a help,' leading us up blind alleys and leaving us in a state of confusion about ourselves. We believe that this is what commonly happens when we try to apply the construct 'reason–emotion' to our experiences. Let us now examine some of the implications of this construct.

It is a compliment to be called rational and something of an insult to be termed 'emotional'. Reason is cool, calm, aloof, while feelings are hot blooded, animal. Some sort of balance between the two is seen as desirable though it is certainly nearer the 'reason' pole of the construct. The superiority of men, with their power of reason, over emotional women reflects this in the popular stereotype of the family. Women's emotionality accompanies what is seen as their nearer horizons, their maternal instincts and defence of their children. While all this is seen as desirable (in a woman) it proves that they need to be looked after, like children or primitive races. Northern European races are, of course, supremely rational, their ice-cold temperaments reflecting the climate. Moving south, you encounter Gallic 'flare', Mediterranean 'hot-headedness' and the 'jungle rhythms' of equatorial people. The myth of the 'noble savage' justifies colonial rule. The ideal Briton is seen as a cheery stoic, armed only with a cricket bat against the fast bowler of fate. His rationality stands in sharp contrast to the passion of women, Latins and animals.

We can see that our use of the construct of reason versus emotion has gone beyond a simple application to our own personal experience – it is a dimension along which we are prepared to place whole nations and which serves to denigrate one half of humankind (women). The two ends of the construct do not carry equal value: that which is rational is revered; the emotional is distrusted and despised. Although everyone is seen as having the capacity for both rational thought and emotions, the latter must be held in check and diverted into harmless activities (in Freud's terms, 'sublimated'), or kept out of conscious awareness (repressed). The idea of repression conjures up an image of pressure building up within the individual, pressure which must be discharged safely (preferably in team games rather than masturbation).

We have written the above in a rather tongue-in-cheek fashion, but it serves to show how we use the reason–emotion construct to separate these aspects of our experience, and how value is attached only to one end of the construct – the 'reason' end. The construct, however, is a poor one, since it implies that the two poles are mutually exclusive. If reason and emotion are polar opposites you can have a compromise, a kind of half-way house, but you cannot have the two poles together. The construct cannot allow that there could be a logic to passion. It tells us to disown our feelings – they are primitive knee-jerks for which we are not responsible (though we should control them). The cost is that we have to accept feelings as irrational – meaning can belong only to events at the other end of the construct. Even though we allow a marginal place for 'women's intuition', we are encouraged to distrust feelings that we cannot articulate and give a good reason for.

While it is no bad thing to call people to account for their actions, it is a mistake to dismiss responses that cannot be articulated verbally and accounted for rationally, the kinds of experiences we call 'gut' reactions. When we try, as individuals, to make sense of the way we respond to events, we automatically refer to the reason–emotion construct as a guiding framework. We are accustomed to asking ourselves what we *think* and what we *feel*. The very existence of these two terms as alternatives in our language reinforces the notion that they refer to separate entities, but a little reflection on this shows that it is not borne out by experience. Ask yourself these questions: Do you feel things 'in a different part of your body from where you have your thoughts? Indeed, is it possible to localise either of these supposedly separate modes of experience? When you are faced with a difficult decision, do your thoughts and your feelings take turns in presenting themselves in your conscious awareness? The idea is ludicrous – what we actually experience is always a mixture of both. In fact it is more than this, for you can have a mixture only of things which are themselves separate. We are arguing that 'thought' and 'feeling' are terms which have been used artificially to divide that which is whole. This is one of the key features of PCP; Kelly could find no advantage in dividing up experience in this way, giving rise to a variety of different 'processes', such as motivation, drive, cognition and emotion (the areas into which psychology is traditionally divided). PCP takes as its unit of study the whole person, and denies that there is any meaningful way of breaking down our psyche into component parts, People are, in this respect, not like machines that one *can* take apart to see how all the bits fit together.

This is not to say the PCP denies the experience we call 'emotion'. But at the heart of the Kellian enterprise is an attempt to understand all human conduct and experience in the same terms, to render it explicable through a single theoretical framework, to avoid the trap of dividing experience up into component parts. What we have come to refer to as 'emotions' Kelly identified as the profound disturbance we feel when we find that our accustomed view of the world, the way we habitually construe it, leaves us totally unprepared for coping with some events. The way we construe our world provides us with a storehouse of plans of action, which are probably never consciously articulated, but nevertheless enable us to anticipate the path we wend through our affairs. When something happens which is beyond the capacity of our constructs to accommodate, when we are faced with events that refuse to fit our mental map of how things are, the ground shakes beneath us. We are forced into a reappraisal of our construing, and if this involves constructs that are central to our general understanding of ourselves and others, there will be a veritable earthquake. What we call emotion Kelly sees as this experience of 'ground shaking', of constructs in transition.

The reason–emotion construct inevitably leads us to feel that we are in conflict; our thoughts seem inconsistent with our feelings, and the value-laden nature of the construct urges us to place more weight on what we have put into the 'rational thought' category, which has further negative pay-offs. It encourages us to think of humans as a mixture of the rational and the irrational. Those aspects of our experience which do not meet the criterion requirements for inclusion in the reason/logic end of the construct are inevitably seen as irrational and illogical. We are so used to this assumption about human nature that it can seem beyond question, but it is a model that encourages us to doubt our judgement, to have no faith in our decision-making efforts. We worry that the unreason of emotion has tainted our cool assessment of the situation.

An alternative to this, and one which we feel offers a more positive and useful construal of human nature, is a PCP approach, the essence of which can be seen if we combine two central features of PCP. First we take as our starting point the whole person. Emotion and reason thus become, for our purposes, irrelevant. The second central feature concerns the way in which constructs are organised within a person. We have already briefly indicated that what gives a person their stamp of individuality is the particular constructs (you could call them questions or theories) they are currently using as a framework with which to make sense of their world. We shall be exploring the nature of constructs more fully in later chapters, but for the moment we need to say something about how these constructs are organised. Kelly saw constructs as having a hierarchical structure, the most important and over-arching ones being at the top (or 'superordinate'). These 'big' constructs themselves subsume a greater number of 'subordinate' constructs, which subsume others, and so on; on paper it would look rather like a family tree. Superordinate constructs are those which are in some way central to a person's approach to themselves and others. An example might be 'good versus evil'. This construct might subsume, among others, the construct 'good friend versus poor friend'. The organisation of these constructs means that this person may take a course of action which they feel implies that they are a 'poor friend' if it is the only way of overcoming a greater 'evil'. Being 'good' (rather than 'evil') is therefore superordinate to being 'a good friend' (rather than a poor one). This is a very simple example, and we apologise for this long-winded account of what seems to be an uncomplicated idea, but the point we are making is that there is a very real logic in the system. (Kelly called this 'psycho-logic' to distinguish it from formal logic. Formal logic would place 'unkind' at the opposite end of the dimension from 'kind', whereas the psycho-logic of an individual's construct system may have 'kind' and 'ruthless' at opposite poles.) There is nothing irrational about the action of the person in our example when we understand the arrangement of their constructs: this is the second central feature that is so important to the reconstrual we are proposing. Whole people behave, act, make decisions, weigh up pros and cons and so on by reference to the internal logic of their own particular construct system. Their decision may not appear logical from the vantage point of their neighbour's system of construing, but it has its own logic nonetheless. PCP thus offers us a way of construing the person without seeing them as irrational and without dividing up their experience in such a way as leads inevitably to feelings of being in a state of conflict. Let us now examine, through some case studies, how the reason–emotion construct leads us into difficulties, and how a PCP approach can help to point the way out of them.

In our first example, we look at one person's apparently irrational response to another.

Stephanie couldn't understand the conflict she experienced when she was with John. Trying to be dispassionate and objective about him, she had to agree that he was a considerate man, polite, eager to please, and always ready to apologise for any inconvenience he caused her. This logical appraisal of him stood in sharp contrast to her feelings, which appeared totally irrational, When she was with him, she felt tense and often snapped at him for no reason. She would look out for any small mistake or clumsiness as an excuse to lose her temper with him. She would find herself waiting for evidence of his unimportant annoying habits and long to take him to task for them. In short, she could not make rational sense of her angry, resentful feelings towards him. She began to see herself as petty, ill tempered and ungenerous, and felt very reproachful towards her irrationality, spending what felt like a lot of energy controlling her feelings.

A close examination of the situation showed that Stephanie had every reason to be irritated by John. On consideration, she felt that his constant apologies were not heartfelt, but a tactic he used to disarm her and prevent her from dealing honestly with him. She had become uncharacteristically self-conscious about her own behaviour. She likened it to playing an opponent at tennis who kept saying 'sorry'. The effect was to make her feel that she could not play *her* shots properly and also had to apologise for the slightest error. The interaction had become a tentative dance. Stephanie felt that in fact John imposed on her a great deal, but prevented her from drawing attention to it. Each instance in itself was trivial, but to her the pattern was clear and unmistakable; he was a Uriah Heap. In her view he was doing something to her – denying her freedom of action. He might not have been aware of what he was doing, and indeed she might have been wrong. The point is that this was her assessment of the relationship, manifested in the irritation which crystallised around any annoying excuse. Once we look past Stephanie's division of her experience into 'rational thought versus irrational emotion', and reconstrue her experience as coherent and rational, the story begins to make sense. Behind every 'gut' feeling is meaning, and it is profoundly unpsychological to deny this.

In the next example, we again look at someone whose feelings are in apparent conflict with their reason, this time concerning a decision they have to make about their future. The example also helps us to illustrate how PCP deals with decision-making.

Colin was happy in his job as accountant in a small local manufacturing business. However, money was tight at home. He began to feel that he ought to be looking for a better-paid job, and he applied for a post in the accounts department of a large advertising company in a nearby city. The post offered prospects for advancement and the immediate reward of more money. He went for interview and was offered the job. However, at this point he found himself wishing that he hadn't got it. He became depressed at the thought of leaving his present job and could not whip up any enthusiasm for the new one. His upset and embarrassment were further confounded by the constant congratulations of his colleagues. To them, it seemed, the move was entirely sensible. In the face of the apparent logic of the decision to accept the new post, Colin could make no sense of his feelings. He berated himself as irrational, indecisive and a 'born worrier'. But to truly understand the meaning of his reaction, we must reconstrue his feelings as logical and look at what work was about for Colin.

Objectively, he saw work in terms of money and promotion, but there was also a social side to it that he had taken for granted. He liked the people he worked with, and found them refreshingly accepting and uncompetitive. Although he didn't socialise much with them outside work, the working day itself was often punctuated by little social interludes and interesting conversation. There was always a sympathetic ear available, and a general air of easy camaraderie. In short, Colin felt he was 'on the same wavelength' as his workmates, and the friendship they gave him was an important feature of the job, although until now it had always appeared as 'ground' rather than 'figure' for him.

The problem was that the job wasn't very well paid, and everyone else around him, especially his family, seemed to feel that the prime issues were most definitely money and prospects. He pondered over his dilemma and finally decided to accept the new job, but he did not find this an occasion for self-congratulation. That he had experienced so much heartache over a choice that a more rational being would have found obvious seemed to him to be evidence of his indecisiveness and irrationality. He had ended up doing what he felt he ought to do rather than what he wanted to do, and saw it as a final victory for head over heart. It was because he felt he could not put forward a rational argument to defend the decision that his feelings urged (staying in his present job) that he saw this course of action as ultimately irrational and irresponsible. But upon closer examination, we discover the logic of his apparent unreason.

It is often the case that it is not until we are faced with the prospect of losing something that we realise what it means to us and what facets of ourselves have become invested in it. Different kinds of loss may have very different implications, but they always carry meaning. They always raise the implicit question 'how can I carry on being "me" without this?'. And whether we give the answer 'quite easily' or 'with great difficulty' depends upon how much of what is important to us is bound up in that which is lost. When faced with the prospect of 'losing' his job, although he could not articulate it at first, Colin realised that the meaning that his job held for him went beyond considerations of finance and career prospects. Certainly, constructs such as 'well paid versus poorly paid' were among those he used when thinking about work, but it became clear that he had come to construe his working life along many other dimensions that reflected what were for him, important issues. 'Friendly versus detached', 'personal versus impersonal' and 'people-centred versus task-centred' were some of the dimensions he found that he had, without conscious awareness, adopted as signposts on his mental map of working life. They were some of the meanings attached to work for Colin.

Looked at in this way, his dilemma can be rewritten. Rather than seeing him as torn between the dictates of head versus heart, we see him as engaged in a process which Kelly referred to as 'circumspection–pre-emption–control' (the 'CPC cycle'). This means that when we have a decision to make, we take a kind of mental stroll around the landscape of our constructs (circumspection in this sense means 'having a look around'). In this phase of the decision process we are finding out what are, for us, the most important issues, the constructs that are superordinate for us in the area we are dealing with. In this phase, the person asks 'what is ultimately at issue here?' and juggles with relevant dimensions along which the decision outcome is to be judged. Two people faced with objectively the same decision will have different subjective decisions to make; different things are likely to be at issue. Of course, this process is often carried out without verbal articulation of the issues we are weighing up, and we frequently make decisions without experiencing any kind of argument being enacted inside our heads. Sometimes the reverse is true – we almost hear the different sides to the argument, like holding a conversation with ourselves. But the process is the same in either case. The problem is that constructs which are of over-arching importance to us are often those that we never get around to labelling. They are so much a part of the background to the way we think that we are unaware of them. It would be like asking a fish to say what water is. This is one reason why issues that are important to us often surface only as vague feelings, the kind of feelings Colin had when he thought about leaving his job.

In the light of this circumspection, we come to some kind of agreement with ourselves as to what the superordinate issues are in this decision, and this is what Kelly called 'pre-emption'. Here the person decides on his or her priorities. In the job example, the answer might be 'OK, finance is the big thing' or 'No, what is really important is being among friends'. The final phase of the decision, 'control', simply means that we identify (and ultimately take, all other things being equal) the appropriate action: If the issue is money, I'll take the new job' or 'What really counts is people I can talk, to – I'll stay where I am'.

Of course, decisions are rarely this uncomplicated. We also have to take into account what other people want and need, especially if they depend upon us. But the point we are making is that talking in terms of 'heads' and 'hearts' obscures a rational psycho-logical process. Just as there is a logic to passion, the reverse is also true; intense pleasure or pain can accompany so-called rational decisions. Only when we abandon the cognition–emotion construct and talk of human processes in a unified language will our actions begin to make sense.

Part II
The Nature of Personality

The reader should now have a firm grasp of the idea of constructive alternativism and some other facets of PCP. Constructive alternativism remains a key concern throughout the rest of the book, since in each chapter we aim to show (among other things) how a reconstrual of a question, issue, or event can often be facilitative.

In this section we ask the reader to apply the principle of constructive alternativism to the notion of personality. This is a big request to make: the way we think about personality, character, temperament (or whatever label you choose) is another of those constructions that appears to us to be a fact, and trying different perspectives may not be easy. The aim of this section is to show how an alternative construction of personality can be more useful and offer us more understanding of human behaviour and experience than the one to which we are used. We have already said a little about some of these issues in Chapter 1, when we discussed some of the differences between PCP and other psychologies.

We also aim in each chapter to elaborate some more facets of PCP, particularly as they relate to personality. By the end of Part II the reader should have a good idea of how Kelly saw personality, what it is that makes us different from or similar to each other, and how PCP accommodates the process of personal change (although this is dealt with in more detail in the final section of the book).

In the opening chapter we begin the process of reconstruing what we mean by 'personality', and the implications that this has for personal change. The next chapter approaches the issue of individual differences through the vehicle of interpersonal attraction. We put forward Kelly's view that one's personality is constituted by one's own particular, idiosyncratic perspective on events: one's construct system. So it follows that each of us is similar to or different from another person to the extent that our construing, is alike or different.

Chapter 8 confronts basic assumptions underlying traditional concepts of personality. It exposes the metaphors upon which our notion of a stable, unified personality is based, and suggests an alternative construction which helps us to make sense of the times when we feel we are being inconsistent or acting 'out of character'.

In Chapter 9, we turn our attention to the issue of the origins of personality, that is how a person comes to be the way he or she is; and in the final chapter of this section, a Kellian, dynamic view of human nature is contrasted with traditional 'static' views through the question 'Why have you changed?'. We look at how, within a PCP framework, personal change comes about and the implications such change has for the individual and those who share his or her life.

Throughout this section, Kelly's concept of 'anticipation' is a recurrent theme. A person's construct system and the way they anticipate events are part of the same process and cannot be separated.

Chapter 6
Can You Change Your Personality?

This is a question that assumes that we have personalities in the first place. It seems self-evident that we each possess a personality. It accounts for our individuality and our uniqueness; it explains why we don't all act in the same way when confronted with the same event. For example, why does A like parties, fast cars and plenty of friends, while B prefers a quiet life, a few good friends and is shy in the presence of others? Why is it that, when faced with the same frustrating event, say a train being late, one person becomes furious, another is depressed and a third remains unaffected? It seems almost a truism to answer 'because they have different personalities'.

In order to see why we are dealing here with a bad question, we must first appreciate that to conceive of personality in this concrete way is unhelpful. A personality is not a thing or an entity that can be directly observed. You cannot open up a person's body and examine their personality. Personality is what we infer when we observe a person's behaviour. We look at what they do and make inferences about the kind of personality they have on the basis of our observations.

But one problem with this is that people's behaviour is heavily influenced by the particular circumstances of the situation they are dealing with. This is what psychologists mean when they say that behaviour is 'situation-specific' or 'context-specific'. This specificity is a problem for the notion of personality, since personality refers to that which is constant in a person's behaviour. If people behave in a variety of different manners depending on the context, in what sense can they be said to have a personality 'type' which manifests itself in their behaviour?

Despite this problem, it is generally accepted that we do bring to bear our own individual stamp or signature on what we do. The manner in which two of us give to the same charity, vote for the same political party or greet an old friend is likely to be subtly different, and certainly to mean different things to us the actors. The psychology of personality is concerned with such individual differences and is an attempt to understand the uniqueness of a person's character.

There are many competing theories of personality that propose explanations in radically different terms - traits, somatic types, oedipal conflicts, response-reinforcement contingencies, and of course, personal constructs. It is tempting to ask 'which theory is correct?', yet this would be another bad question, since they should not be judged in terms of their truth but their usefulness. In PCP terms, we are using 'true-false' and 'useful-not useful' as dimensions, constructs that we are imposing upon things in order to make sense of them.

Abandoning the idea of 'truth' in this way may sound like a radical departure from accepted ways of thinking. But throughout science, examples can be found of phenomena which it may be useful to construe in a variety of ways. In physics, as we saw earlier, an electron is sometimes considered to be a particle and sometimes a wave. For some purposes it is useful to see it in one way, for some another. In time, a better theory may emerge (say in terms of 'superstrings' that will account for even more phenomena), but in the meantime physicists do not ask 'is an electron *really* a particle or a wave?'; they allow both propositions to exist. These propositions have been invented by physicists to try to account for their observations; they are not facts that have been 'discovered'. In the same way, theories of personality are inventions, not facts. Even the idea that people have personalities is a theory, an invention. It is one way of construing what people do in an attempt to understand their behaviour. And each of these theories should be judged in terms of their usefulness in this attempt.

Personality theories, then, are propositions put forward to help us understand what makes us tick; why we think, feel and act as we do, particularly when we are a problem or a puzzle to ourselves. They are useful if they help us understand the puzzle or solve the problem, and thus perhaps accept or change ourselves in some way that we would like. However, the way we typically view personality, and even the very use of personality-type words in our language (such as 'honest' or 'reliable') has implications. We tend to lose sight of the fact that personality is a construction and not a fact. For example, we might see a mother shouting at her toddler for what seems (to us) a minor misdemeanour. We then say that she is impatient or that she has no patience. Our language has deceived us into thinking of patience as an entity that people have a certain quantity of, and we are left with the problem of where we get this patience from.

Patience, in this example, represents a trait, i.e. any relatively enduring way in which one individual differs from another. Other examples of traits are generosity, cruelty and dependency. Most people, including some psychologists, are confirmed trait theorists, that is, they use the idea of personality traits in thinking about and explaining people's behaviour (including their own). The point about explanation is important: not only are traits seen as a kind of shorthand *description* for the 'consistencies' we notice in a person's behaviour, like always being kind to animals or losing one's temper easily in an argument, but they are also used as *explanations* of that behaviour. We are seduced by our own language into the belief that when we call someone 'patient' we are not simply describing how they commonly behave, but are also accounting for that behaviour by implying that they 'have' an inner, hidden quality which manifests itself in their behaviour. Yet there is a fatal circularity in this argument. If we say that a man is aggressive because he hits others, we are not justified in using what is only our own inference ('aggressive') as a causal explanation for that same behaviour. In effect we can never refute our theory. We ask 'why do you say that John is aggressive?' and answer 'because he often ends up in a fight'. We then ask 'why does he often end up in a fight?' and reply 'because he is aggressive'. If we have laboured this point, it is because it is important to understand the difference between a description and an explanation, and to appreciate the dangers in confusing them. The way that this has been problematic for personality theory is that we have lumbered ourselves with the notion that traits exist within us and account for the way we behave. It is no accident that most personality theories have been generated in the world of the clinician, who commonly sees people who are dissatisfied with and puzzled by themselves. What they want is a way of changing, not simply a diagnosis or a description of their personalities. But we all frequently find that our behaviour and experience are a mystery to both ourselves and others, and the desire to change is usually accompanied by the pessimistic belief that 'you can't change your personality'.

It is not difficult to understand this, in view of the way in which the question is posed. After all, we are bound to think of ourselves in the same way as we think about others, in terms of traits that we are stuck with in much the same way as our height or the shape of our nose. Furthermore, we tend to carry on believing in this theory of ourselves, even when there is evidence against it. For example, I may see myself as a 'clumsy' person, but when I do perform tasks efficiently and dextrously, I see this more as good luck than good management.

When a person has a theory about how things or people work, then evidence which confirms the theory occupies the foreground of their awareness, while counter-evidence is often ignored or not even noticed. It is small wonder that we feel we cannot change our personalities if evidence of dexterity doesn't rock the 'clumsiness' theory, but is seen as just luck.

This idea of the permanence of our personality characteristics reinforces our notion of the 'depth' of personality. We come to see our behaviour as some kind of 'surface' phenomenon, while 'personality' lies somewhere underneath. This is why we can feel that any change we may bring about in our *behaviour*, without any corresponding change in our *personality*, is nothing but pretence.

In short, then, most people (including some psychologists) are trait theorists. They believe that they have a personality comprising a set of traits which remains more or less stable and constant, despite the fact that their behaviour and reactions differ according to the occasion. This personality is seen as probably being present at birth, and although it may be influenced strongly by events in childhood. It sets like concrete, and by the time you reach adulthood, you're stuck with it. Because this theory is widely held, and we are all to some extent prisoners of other people's expectations and descriptions, we find it hard to see ourselves as able to change. Thus the theory is reinforced.

Nevertheless, most of us keep alive the hope that maybe we *can* change. Examples occasionally come to light of people who claim to be dramatically changed by a love affair, hypnosis, psychotherapy, or having narrowly escaped death. Like the adverts that show 'before' and 'after' photos of people who have shed five stones in weight, we highlight these rare examples as evidence that maybe we too can be 'born again'. Perhaps we can begin at last to act on all that good advice: 'don't worry – what good did worrying ever do?' 'just be confident in yourself, you're as good as anybody else' – advice that is so easy to give and yet so hard to follow. Why can some people apparently change their personalities when I find it so hard to change mine?

PCP suggests we look at personality not in terms of collections of traits, but rather in terms of the way we construe, i.e. the particular questions with which we approach our social world and the theories that each of us silently constructs about that world.

It is important here to ensure that we are not misled into substituting 'constructs' for 'personality' in any simple way. We do not 'have' constructs in the same way that people generally accept that we 'have' personalities. We 'have' constructs only in the same way as we 'have' questions. The important difference is that 'having a question' does not preclude the possibility of learning to ask a different question. To say that I have the construct 'patient versus impatient' makes it sound as though it is a feature of my psychological make-up which cannot help but be revealed through my behaviour. This is just trait theory in disguise. Rather than talk of a construct as something we have, it is more true to the spirit of PCP to say that construing is something we *do* and which therefore could be done differently.

The implications for personal change are immense. Once we set aside our trait theories, we begin to focus more closely on what we *do* rather than on what we *are*. Thus, rather than seeing myself as an impatient person (who is just made that way and cannot change) I can say that sometimes I *act* impatiently, which leaves open the possibility that I may act differently tomorrow. And to say that 'I am impatient' or that 'I have no patience' implies that you can expect less of me than would be the case if I were 'acting impatiently'.

The language of PCP allows us to be optimistic about change. We *can* look at things differently, we *can* start to ask different questions. But this does not mean that all we have to do is find an alternative construction of our world that we like the look of (say, seeing yourself as capable of assertiveness) and unproblematically adopt it. Starting to construe the world in a different way may well be difficult and carry in its wake various implications we hadn't bargained for, as we shall see later.

PCP proposes that it is helpful to understand the differences between people primarily in terms of the different ways in which they perceive their world. This is what guides our conduct, feelings and thought (or 'processes' as Kelly referred to them). Rather than thinking of people as though they are collections of traits, habits or defences, the proposition is that we should think of people as scientists, constantly engaged in building and testing theories about their social world. The answer to questions like 'Why did she do that?' thus come via an understanding of that person's idiosyncratic theories, how they were developed, the 'experiments' the person is prepared to test them with, and what they are prepared to accept as evidence.

Let us imagine that we have just met a man for the first time. Afterwards we all agree on one thing – we did not like him much. Words like 'surly', aggressive' and 'big-headed' are advanced to sum him up. These words describe his behaviour, but do not tell us *why* he acts as he does. For an explanation of this we have to try to put ourselves in his shoes, see the world through his eyes, conjure up his theories, know something of his history and particularly what sense he has made of that history. Perhaps he does not feel as cocky as he looks, but divides people into two sorts – winners and losers, wolves and sheep, those who seize life's opportunities and wring concessions from a hard world, and those who whine and are preyed upon. Given such a theory of life, the options available to him are clear. The way he construes determines the range of options he sees as open to him. We cannot forecast what, in his terms of 'winner or loser', he will turn out to be, but his way of construing limits his range of alternatives and we should not be surprised if he opted to be a 'winner' if this were at all possible.

After a superficial acquaintance with him, we may be puzzled. 'What's in it for him?' we may think. 'He certainly can't have any friends, for the way he treats people is appalling!' But from his point of view, the most important thing is not to show weakness, but to show people you are not scared of them, to spit the world in the eye. As a result he may feel lonely, and regret this, but for him this is the price that simply has to be paid for being one of life's 'winners'.

The next question is of course 'Can people look at things differently?' It will become clear from our example that acting in a radically different way depends upon seeing the world in different terms. If this man is beaten into submission, meets a faster gun so to speak, he may come to construe himself as a loser rather than a winner. This may entail drastic changes in behaviour but it will leave his major construction intact: the world is still divided into two sorts of people. All he has done is to move from one end of his construct to the other, like a coin rolling up and down in a slot. In fact Kelly referred to this as 'slot rattling'. This man's problem is not to see himself as rather more of a loser than he had previously, but to develop new constructs, new ways of looking at his world, which do not entail dividing people into winners and losers. But the new ways of construing also need to enable him to retain what he values of his old self (such as strength, resolution and determination). He needs to find a way of construing which allows him to hold on to these but does not commit him to a bullish personal style and its attendant social isolation.

The problem here is that to all of us the way *we* see things seems natural to *us* – it is the way things *are*. We all have a lot invested in our theories, however much bother they cause us, and we are not likely to change them whimsically. However inadequate, our theories enable us to carry on dealing with others, give us ground rules to help us anticipate and carry on a social life, and the prospect of throwing away our theory, no matter how difficult it makes our life, is deeply disturbing to us. In fact Kelly advanced a new definition of hostility – 'the attempt by someone to cling to a theory that has already been proved to be untenable'.

There are many difficulties in changing what is referred to as 'our personality'. We fear what we may lose of ourselves if we change in the way we desire to change. Thus many of these difficulties are perhaps better thought of not as an inability to change, but as a reluctance to endure the losses we imagine are implied by the change we desire. We should not ask 'how can I change my personality?' but instead 'how can I act differently?'. Rephrasing the question does not solve all our problems, but at least we are asking fruitful questions to which we are more likely to find answers.

In the next chapter, using the vehicle of interpersonal attraction, we explore more fully the idea of what 'personality' meant for Kelly and in what sense we can fruitfully see people as similar to or different from each other.

Chapter 7
Do Opposites Attract?

Perhaps one of the most puzzling questions which we often pose ourselves is 'What is it that we find attractive in another person?'. We often answer this for ourselves when it comes to examining our own relationships, e.g. 'We have a lot in common' or 'I like her sense of humour', but this doesn't really explain the attraction. And when it comes to accounting for the relationships that our friends choose we are often at a loss. We say 'I don't know what he sees in her' and 'I wouldn't have thought he was her type', and yet people obviously do not choose their partners/mates and their friends randomly. Of course there is a fairly strong 'opportunity' factor; we tend to get to know best the people who live near to us, work with us or whom we meet because of a common interest, so this narrows down the field a bit. But even so, within this immediate social circle, we find people we are attracted to more than others.

The common sayings reflect our attempts to try to account for people's choices – we say 'like marries like', and contrariwise 'opposites attract' (like magnets). Most psychologists, probably sensing that this is something of a minefield, have ignored this paradox, or have settled for a version of 'like marries like' by examining the social, educational and cultural backgrounds of married couples. The best we seem able to come up with is that people are most likely to choose as a partner someone who has had a similar educational background, whose class origins are similar to their own, and who is of the same religion and culture.

Well, perhaps people who are similar to each other do find each other attractive, or perhaps it is the other way around – people with 'opposing' personality characteristics find each other irresistible. We can certainly frequently find evidence for both of these theories of interpersonal attraction if we look amongst our friends and relatives, and indeed, there is a temptation to look at couples who, in our eyes, are obviously very dissimilar, and to decide that they are 'opposite' simply because they do not appear to be similar. But frequently neither explanation fits and we are left feeling baffled by the apparently mysterious phenomenon of attraction.

Let us now examine why this question and its converse, 'does like attract like?' is a bad one, and why it cannot help us to understand what it is that one person sees in another.

The way that many psychologists would try to settle the issue is by looking at a large number of people who, say, had recently decided to get married. They would assess each individual on a number of tests designed to measure one or more aspects of their personality, such as how 'extraverted' or 'introverted' they are, whether they are dominant rather than submissive, authoritarian, or have neurotic tendencies. These personality assessments would then be compared to see how similar or different the pairs were in general. This seems like a logical thing to do (if you're a psychologist!). The problem is we are all too likely to find no clear general relationship between the personalities of people who find each other attractive – here we again come up against the concept of personality, which we have met already in earlier chapters. In order to measure something it has to exist first! When we 'measure' such things as 'extraversion' or 'neuroticism' we are assuming that these things exist in some concrete way inside each of us, and that anyone, given the right tools (e.g. a personality inventory) can find out how much we 'have' of a variety of personality characteristics. It is then only a small step to comparing individuals to see how much they have relative to each other.

We suggested in the last chapter that we do not 'have' personality in the sense that we 'have' brown hair or a crooked nose, but that what 'characterises' us, i.e. gives a familiar theme to the way we behave, the views we express and so on, are the constructs that we are currently using, the questions with which we habitually approach social situations. As we have pointed out already, one major difference in this approach is that it has a much more facilitative attitude to personal change ('personalities' tend to seem fixed, but one can learn to 'ask different questions', i.e. alter one's construct system), but another important difference is that people who are similar in that they have similar questions about their social world may behave and appear quite differently.

Let us take as an example a young man; one of the major constructs that he uses in his social encounters is creative-practical. So when he meets people and starts to get to know them, the question he implicitly asks is 'Is this person creative or practical?'. Let us suppose he visits the home of a young woman he has recently met and finds that she is something of a DIY enthusiast – there are shelves on the walls and he arrives in the kitchen in time to see his new acquaintance unblocking the drain. This is likely to seem strong evidence that she is 'practical' rather than 'creative' in terms of our man's construct. He will probably then set this up as something of a working hypothesis and test it out on future occasions to see if he is correct. He meets his acquaintance again, who tells him that she has just finished rewiring the house. The construct is further validated by this new evidence. Remember that in no way are we suggesting that 'practical' and 'creative' should become part of the way we view 'personality', but rather that the practical–creative dimension is important in the way *this* young man looks at other people and himself. It is a question he is constantly posing.

Let us now imagine that he views himself as 'creative' rather than practical'. He is something of an amateur artist, occasionally writes music, and is reluctant to tackle practical tasks around the house. But a problem he has always found in his social relationships is in finding someone who seemed to understand his point of view. Even people who seemed to him extremely 'creative' would hint that there is no reason why he shouldn't try to change a blown fuse in a plug. They didn't seem to understand that creative people simply can't be practical as well. And trying to be more practical would, in his mind, involve 'giving up' many of the things he prizes in his creativity. However, this girl he has just met seems different from other people in his social world. Right from the start she seemed to understand him, and seemed to see things the way he did. She described herself as a highly practical and down-to-earth person. Although she admired creativity in others, she felt she was too much of a 'realist' to be creative and really preferred to have her feet firmly on the ground.

These two people don't have what we would call, in common parlance, a lot in common – to the outsider they appear as different as chalk and cheese – but are they really 'opposites'? What they *do* have in common is something much more important – a similar way of construing people. They both ask the question 'Is he or she creative or practical?'. The fact that they have each opted for opposite ends of the construct in how they see themselves is immaterial. The reason why they get on so well is that they can understand the other's perspective on the world. From an objective point of view then, asking whether he 'is' creative or she 'is' practical and whether they have 'opposing' personalities, is a bad question. The important thing is that he construes himself as 'creative' and her as 'practical' on a creative–practical dimension which is the foundation stone of all his dealings with people. The fact that she too uses the same construct is the basis for their mutual appeal, and not any objective similarity or dissimilarity in their personalities.

So the first point we have made is that it is more meaningful to talk about similarities between people by referring to similarities in their construing than to any objective assessment of their personalities. However, the fact that social relationships are essentially dynamic phenomena, constantly being 'created' between two people, means that the story does not end here. This leads us to another clue as to why we might come to see couples as comprising two opposites. We get some notion of this when we look at our own children, especially if we have two. We, often hear people say 'You wouldn't think they had the same parents, they're so different', 'He's always in trouble for one thing or another, but we never have any trouble with her', 'The elder one is very quiet – she just sits and reads most of the time, but the younger one is just the opposite – always running and shouting with her mates'. This is something that most of us who have some experience of children can identify with, and is a clue to how children, and adults, can come to see themselves and be seen by others as opposites in a pair. For it would be just *too* coincidental for children in a family to just happen to have 'opposite' personalities – these young people are doing something (for Kelly, people are always actively engaged in encountering their social world and trying to make sense of it). What is happening here is a kind of carving up of the personality territory – it's almost as if there isn't room in one family for two boisterous children or two troublesome children or two sensible children. Given some small difference between them in the way they are perceived by their parents, children begin to move towards an occupation of different ends of these dimensions. so that a child who begins to be seen as rather more quiet than his or her brother or sister comes to occupy the role of 'the quiet one' and the sibling becomes 'the noisy one'.

When we look at adult partnerships, we can see that this concept has some explanatory value here too: rather than people of widely differing psychological make-up becoming attracted to each other, the reverse is likely to be true to some extent – couples appear as psychological opposites by the way they come to divide up the 'character territory' between them.

So the questions 'Do opposites attract?' and 'Does like attract like?' really have no sensible answers, for they are the result of a concept of personality which we find unhelpful, in many respects, for our understanding of people and why they do the things they do. Only when we begin to think of personality in terms of the questions people characteristically bring with them to social situations do we find a way of fruitfully examining the apparent mysteries of interpersonal attraction.

pter 8

at am I Really Like?

Pick up a pile of old magazines from any period in the past 20 years or so, and it is a fair bet that one of them will feature a questionnaire or quiz of the 'get-to-know-what-you're-really-like' type. Many of us, perhaps more so than we would like to admit, feel at least a modest degree of curiosity to read the questions, choose the reply we feel most typifies us, and then greedily scan the answer section, probably with a sense of rising indignation that they have got it all wrong. Like a horoscope, if it doesn't fit, at least we can say it is only a bit of fun.

But displays of curiosity such as this say something about the way we feel about ourselves. There is a lurking suspicion that perhaps we don't know ourselves very well, that our thoughts, feelings and actions are sometimes a mystery to us, even though at the same time we can't help feeling that no one knows and understands us quite the way *we* do! The temptation to have it all explained by the 'expert' (psychologist, psychiatrist, therapist and so on) is often irresistible. Why should it be that we are open to the implied suggestion that we don't, perhaps can't, *really* know ourselves, and that the magazine questionnaire is at least as good a guide to our personality as our own self-knowledge?

The first reason is one that we met in the previous two chapters. We are part of a culture which has come to see 'personality' as a concrete structure, something that exists in an almost palpable form inside one's body, or at least inside one's 'mind' (whatever that may turn out to be). And we have come to accept the notion that psychologists, by virtue of their expert knowledge, can measure how much of each personality trait we carry within us. We implicitly accept the notion that such insights are available only through the 'trick' questions of the personality inventory – we have to be duped into revealing what we are 'really' like.

It will be clear from the earlier chapters that we do not hold with such a view of personality, that 'what am I like?' is a question more fruitfully

51

answered by examining the constructs with which we habitually approach our social world.

However, a second important reason for our apparent lack of insight into our *real* selves is the experience we all have from time to time that our behaviour, thoughts or feelings (or all three) are inconsistent. We often cannot make sense of what we do, think and feel in terms of the person we hold ourselves to be. If you *really* love your mother, why do you sometimes wish she lived in Australia? If you're *really* so honest, why do you lie to your children about death ('it never happens under the age of 90')? If you *really* want to be liked by X, why do you find yourself acting coldly towards him? Sometimes we can bring forth rational arguments and justifications for these inconsistencies, and these arguments are important to us not simply to convince society that, deep down, we are really acting consistently, but also to reassure ourselves. 'I do really love my mother – it's because I do that she has such power to anger me.' 'I am basically honest, but sometimes that means being cruel, and I can't face doing that to my children.'

But sometimes we are at a loss to find any reasonable (to us) explanations that would satisfy ourselves or others as to the stability and consistency of our character. The problem is that the way we think about personality brings with it the requirement that we present to the world (and to ourselves) a character which is unified, internally consistent and coherent. If we look at ourselves as if we had a certain number of different traits that determine our behaviour, this makes it difficult to understand how an 'extravert' can sometimes act in an 'introverted' way, or why a 'kind' person should act unkindly or have unkind thoughts, and so on.

Adolescents and young adults feel particularly keenly this invisible pressure to come up with some reliable version of 'who I am'. Indeed, writers of self-help books and many psychologists have talked of adolescence as the time of 'finding out who you are'. This promotes the idea that if you search long and hard enough you will find the answer. The idea that we *discover* ourselves, our personalities, permeates our thinking. But the important point is that adolescents, more so than most adults, are busily engaged in a process of trying out different ways of being, and the task they are set, it appears to them, is to draw some conclusions from their widely differing and inconsistent feelings and experiences, about the kind of person they *really* are – no wonder they are often confused.

As adults, our problem is epitomised by the plight of the adolescent. We feel we must choose, must decide on the kind of person we really are. Am I quiet or boisterous? Practical or intellectual? Kind or ruthless? (The shrewd reader will already have recognised these as constructs.)

So we have a problem – how to resolve the observed inconsistencies in ourselves while desperately holding on to a consistent and unified story of 'the kind of person I am'. We sometimes attempt to do this by saying 'I get on with some people better than others – of course I'm different with X compared to when I'm with Y. Quite often we explain the differences in our behaviour in different social situations by saying that sometimes we put on an act in order to make the interaction run smoothly. In this case we are accounting for the difference between our behaviour and what we feel we are really like 'deep down'.

What are we doing when we talk of what we are really like 'deep down'? The notion of personality that this implies is that each of us comprises layers, some deeper and some more superficial than others, and that it is only the 'deep' structures that correspond to the 'real' person. The rest constitute, to greater or lesser degrees, an act which is put on for the benefit of smooth social interactions. Students of human nature have often characterised humankind as comprising a thin, fragile veneer of socialisation which covers a deeper, seething animal instinct. Hermann Hesse's novel *Steppenwolf* and Freud's id and ego are but two examples of the attempt to describe this common human experience.

But If we look hard at this idea, we realise that what we have is not a description of personality as it truly is. We cannot open up a person and observe these hypothetical layers. What we are doing is using a metaphor. We are looking at people as if they were comprised of such layers. What this is, then, is a *theory*, and as such we must judge its success at making sense of what people do. Constructive alternativism, the keystone of PCP, insists that we always remember that there is an infinite number of ways of construing events, some more useful than others. The 'depth' metaphor in personality is one such construal, but it is not the only possible one. The alternative recommended by Kelly is that we approach people 'as if' they were scientists, constantly engaged in testing out hypotheses in their social world. It is another way of construing people, an alternative metaphor.

The stumbling block of the depth metaphor is that it creates problems for people when they try to understand inconsistencies in their behaviour, thoughts and feelings. Let us illustrate this point with an example.

Bill was a person who felt very strongly about violence. He hated it. He abhorred aggression in any form and felt disgust when he observed it in others or in himself. He would never (or hoped he would never) want to inflict pain or distress on another person, and was strongly pacifist in his views. And yet he was fascinated by all things military. Even as an adult he preserved his childhood collection of toy soldiers, and was passionately interested in the details of combat and strategy. The only way it seemed to him that he could make sense of this contradiction was to conclude that 'deep down', underneath his 'peaceful veneer', he was in truth a barbarian. This tormented him and he constantly doubted his faith in his pacifist view of himself.

For Bill, the cost of the 'depth' metaphor in personality was self-doubt and feelings of conflict and guilt. This kind of inner dialogue and the feelings it invokes will be familiar to most of us.

However, once we acknowledge. that what we have in the depth metaphor is just that, and not a fact of human nature, we are free to adopt alternative constructions that may be more helpful. One such construction has been put forward by the construct theorist Miller Mair (1977). He recommends that a more fruitful metaphor is to view ourselves as if we were a 'community of selves'. This community is made up of a collection of often very different people, but they have enough in common for them to be linked together as a whole unit, in the same way that communities in towns or, villages comprise different individuals who share a common ground and a common interest.

Sometimes we are unable to see the common ground that our community stands upon because our view of the overall construct system we operate is clouded by relatively small-scale inconsistencies. In the previous section we talked about superordinate and subordinate constructs and how they are organised. Relatively subordinate or lower-order constructs may appear to present inconsistency, but our superordinate constructs, the all-embracing rules by which we live our lives, confer an order upon things. We can see what this means if we go back to one of our earlier examples. Let us take another look at the mother we described, who feels dishonest about not facing her children with the facts about death. We can make sense of her behaviour when we understand that her construct 'honest versus dishonest' stands in a relatively subordinate position to her construct 'cruel versus kind'. In its turn, this construct will sometimes be subordinated to the demands of yet more superordinate constructions, say 'loving parent versus one who couldn't care less'.

When people feel in conflict about their 'real' self, Mair suggests that they think creatively about the sort of community that might best characterise them, with the hope that they may come to recognise their own differing psychological processes. It may well be that in our desperate attempts to be consistent we are stifling voices in us that insist on being heard, one way or another. Here is an example, in the form of a case study, to illustrate how this can be useful.

Carol, perhaps because she was a student of political sciences, saw herself as suffering from a 'tyranny of democracy', rather like the British parliamentary system. The party in power, with a working majority, managed to get its way despite the fact that the nation was by no means united. There was a vocal opposition which had no say in the executive, and there were minor parties with coherent policies who apparently never had a hope of influencing domestic or foreign policy. Such a metaphor enabled Carol to listen to different aspects of herself. Her 'government' had decided on appeasement. She felt increasingly imposed upon and in need of assertiveness, especially at work. Yet she occasionally had uncontrollable tempers (usually with her children) and her sulkiness at home did not seem to fit with her 'characteristic' cheerfulness. She wondered what she was really like. But the parliamentary metaphor enabled her to realise that this was an impossible question. After all, what did the British people *really* feel about Iraq? Certainly not everyone agreed with government policy!

Seeing ourselves as communities helps us to get away from the depth metaphor, and relieves us of the need to rationalise away inconsistencies. We can begin to allow each member of our community to have his or her say. If we become adept at construing ourselves in this way, we find we are able to allow expression to the selves we find most troublesome to own, perhaps by 'taking it out for a walk on the lead'. In this way we need not feel puzzled or threatened by what we imagine are hidden forces welling up from the depths, and which we feel powerless to control.

The 'community of selves' metaphor can also give us a better understanding of the concept of 'role'. There are two aspects to the 'depth' metaphor – the 'real' self which is deep down and hidden, and the superficial veneer of our 'social' selves. If there is a 'real self' deep down, all the rest is pretence, an act. We are simply acting out roles which bear little relation to our real selves. The power of the depth metaphor is such that we equate role playing with the superficiality of pretence. But if you listen to any good actor talking about what it is like to play a role, it is clear that 'pretending' is a poor description. Rather than pretending to be someone else, the actors' experiences are of finding some aspect of themselves that they can bring to the fore, elaborate and give voice to temporarily.

We are all engaged daily in playing a variety of different roles-work roles, domestic roles, numerous hats that we wear to suit the occasion, and none of these can be described as pretence. In what sense do I 'pretend' to be a mother when I am at home with my children and do all the usual things with them that mothers do with their children? In what sense do I 'pretend' to be a lecturer when I talk to a group of students? These questions clearly seem inappropriate, and yet my behaviour, my demeanour, and even the kind of person I feel myself to be, varies with the particular role I am adopting. Looked at from a PCP point of view, the essence of 'role playing' is giving voice or expression to a particular member of our various selves, to one of the community.

What this illustrates brings us full circle, back to an issue with which we began this chapter. Through the acting out of our many roles, through the elaboration of different aspects of ourselves, we do not 'discover' the kind of person we really are. Instead the process is more like one of being continually engaged in the *creation* of ourselves. We are constantly inventing ourselves in the course of our interactions with others, In this sense, then, personality is not to be found *within* people, but *between* them.

Chapter 9
What Made Me the Way I Am?

Part of the uniqueness of human beings, which sets them apart from other animals, is that they can reflect upon themselves. They are 'self-conscious'. This reflection is manifested whenever we look at ourselves and ask 'Why am I like this?'. Most people at some time in their lives look back on their life to date and ponder on the events and experiences which have made them the kind of people they are. For some troubled individuals this question is never far from their thoughts. We are sometimes gripped by the notion that, just as diseases are better cured when their cause is understood, if we can only discover the events underlying our present difficulties, we may be in a better position to solve them. This is, of course, the basis of many psychological approaches. We may wonder whether something in the way our parents brought us up gave rise to the feelings of inadequacy we suffer. Or whether a long-forgotten traumatic encounter with a dog taught us to fear dogs throughout the rest of our lives. We look back into the past and dredge up memories of events and experiences which, it seems to us, help us to explain to ourselves the way we are.

The very fact that we do enquire into the origins of our personality as we see it is a testimony to our need to make some sense of ourselves in terms of our past, our history. This sense-making is something we *do*: it is an active, constructive process. This is what is meant by 'constructivism', and we argue that it is another essentially human endeavour. It is part of what it means to be a human being, and it is the framework against which we do all our perceiving. It gives meaning to our world – without it, the world would indeed be the 'booming, buzzing confusion' that William James thought described the sensory experience of the newborn infant. We shall first take a look at how this 'sense-making' is manifested in general perception, and then go on to see how this applies to our search for past causes of our present predicament. Finally, we shall show how this search can be a misleading enterprise, and put forward a Kellian proposal concerning the role of the past in our lives.

Constructivism in the Psychology of Perception

One of the things that can be puzzling when we start to look at the nature of perception in humans is that two people will not necessarily agree on what it is they see when they are presented with identical stimuli. And the stimulus can look different to the same person on different occasions. If our perceptual apparatus simply 'records' information from our environment, then assuming that everyone has the same equipment (like a video camera) and that it isn't faulty, we should all 'see' the same things. Why don't we?

Psychologists now generally agree that perception is not a simple and straightforward act of collecting information through our senses. Although they may argue about the level at which this occurs, there is general agreement that perception involves giving *meaning* to the objects of our perception. This process is the basis of many 'projective tests' such as the Rorschach, so-called 'ink-blot', test. There is an assumption underlying such tests that individuals will see different things in an abstract shape, depending on the meaning with which they imbue it. Most people are now familiar with the 'reversing figures' that appear, for example, sometimes as a vase and sometimes as two silhouettes. The stimulus remains the same, but the meaning determines what we see. In one perception experiment, people were presented with the following display, in which the figures rotated and moved from one side of a screen to the other.

When asked 'What do you see?', they typically answered 'The triangle is chasing the circle'. What these people perceived was a result of the meaning with which they had imbued the stimulus.

Gestalt psychologists took up this 'meaningful' aspect of perception and put forward the idea that perception is constructive in its nature, i.e. we actively construct our perceptions from the visual array available to us, and that we do this in such a way as to make a meaningful whole of the stimulus material. This often entails psychologically 'filling in' bits of the perception which are missing. For example, when presented with a pattern of dots like this:

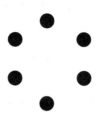

and asked what they see, most people would say not 'six dots', but 'a circle'. They have filled in the gaps in order to make a meaningful whole. Sometimes this also involves deciding which bits of information to select and which to discard. Anyone looking at the night sky and studying the stars will wonder how the original observers ever saw a plough or a great bear in a particular group of stars. In fact, the very notion of a 'group' of things testifies to our predisposition to organise and make sense of our world in a meaningful, patterned way.

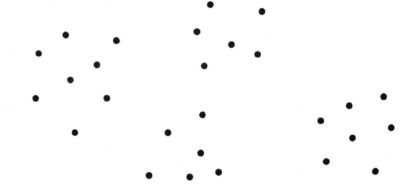

The above can be said to be no more than a random display of dots on a page; however, to us it appears that there are undeniably four 'groups'.

The Gestalt psychologists went rather further than this and suggested that some perceptions constituted 'good gestalts' (like the circle) and some were poorer, or weaker in their organisation. But we shall not here go further than to note that some kind of organising, sense-making and meaningful effort has long been recognised as a fundamental part of our perceptual processes.

Sense-making and 'Causality' in Social Perception

This organisational, sense-making aspect of our psychology is not, we argue, confined to the physical senses; it is present also in our perceptions of other people, events and situations, and of course ourselves. We try to 'make sense' of what other people do and say, to see patterns and themes in their behaviour (this is what we do when we talk about 'personality') and we also do this with ourselves. We try to make sense of and find patterns in our own lives, and one of the ways we do this is to organise our history into some kind of sequence of events that makes sense to us, explaining the kind of person we feel ourselves to be. Essentially, we search the past for the causes of our present.

In this search, we begin from the assumption that a chain of events must have been set in motion, rather like Newton's cradle, and we search further and further back in time for the 'precipitating' event, such as the traumatic event or childhood experience we mentioned earlier. What we are doing here is to take a physical law, that of causality, and transpose it to the realm of the psyche. We are virtually saying 'physical events can let us treat the realm of psychology as if it were like the physical world and try to explain its phenomena in the same way'. Thus we are essentially looking at people as if they were machines. Machines function by the action of forces and the transfer of energy from one component to another in a causal chain. By looking at people in this way we are adopting a metaphor, that is, regarding people as if they were machines and looking for the 'causes' of their preceding events and forces. To the extent that this metaphor is now very entrenched in the way we commonly think about human beings (we talk about being 'run down' like a clock, or 'letting off steam' like Stephenson's *Rocket* it is what Sarbin (1986) has called a 'root metaphor' – a metaphor which has become so fundamental to the way we think about ourselves that we rarely, if ever, notice that this is what we are doing.

So far, then, we have pointed to the endeavour to make sense of our 'self' and its history, and have suggested that the way in which we commonly do this is by looking for causes. But this way of searching for meaningfulness, for a pattern, in our life-events often leads us into difficulties and false judgements. We can begin to understand the formation of myths, superstitions and misconceptions through our attempts to find the 'causes' of events. Not so long ago, a woman who gave birth to a child with a hare lip might have attributed the deformity to having seen a hare during pregnancy. Or we might look at what happened just before an event to explain it; for example, if we see a magpie just before an accident occurs, the accident may become associated in our minds with the antecedent event of seeing a magpie, and the superstition surrounding the magpie, that seeing a single magpie brings bad luck, is thus perpetuated.

These beliefs may seem obviously erroneous to us, but we nevertheless continue to employ the same kind of logic in our own search for the causes of things. Our theories may be more sophisticated (such as that events *distant* in time, say a psychological trauma in childhood, can cause problems later in life) but we employ the notion of causality in just the same way. So in our search for causes we often see relationships between events that are in reality unconnected. But when it comes to looking for psychological explanations of events, we are on even shakier ground. We are used to the notion of causality – it is part of our understanding of many things in the physical world, especially machines, where a force or energy triggers off a series of events which are linked in a causal chain. What we do when we look for psychological causes is to take this machine-like model and apply it to ourselves. We do this quite readily when events in our bodies, such as illness, need explaining. We look for the cause in terms of viruses, germs, etc. We are accustomed to a mechanistic view of our bodies. We have taken this further and said to ourselves 'if bodily events can be understood and explained in terms of cause and effect, like the operation of a machine, maybe the mind works that way too'. So we have adopted the mechanistic metaphor and applied it to our psychological processes.

But there are good reasons to believe that a causal view of things is often not very helpful when it comes to explaining even physical, bodily events; for example, the notion of 'specific aetiology' in illness has been seriously questioned. We argue that we are making unwarranted and unhelpful assumptions when we try to use the same model to try to explain our psychology, to answer questions such as 'What made me the way I am?'. We can see these assumptions underlying many traditional psychological perspectives, which may appear radically different in other ways. For example, psychoanalytical theories try to explain adults' problems in terms of the effect that events early in life had upon the person. Those events are seen as the causes of the problem. (An additional assumption in this tradition is that childhood experiences have a more dramatic and far-reaching effect upon our psyche than our experiences as young adults or middle-aged people. A brief reflection on our own lives, however, would lead us seriously to question this. Many would agree that events such as marriage, parenthood and retirement can herald the most dramatic changes in ourselves.)

Conditioning theories, while differing radically from psychoanalytical ones in their eschewing of 'mentalistic' concepts, still rely upon the explanatory value of past events as causes of present ones. Both types of theory thus see human beings as 'formed' by their experiences. Our attempts to answer the question 'What made me the way I am?' within these perspectives are directed toward looking back on our lives and trying to discover the causes of our present state in the events of the recent or distant past.

Causality in Developmental Psychology

These kinds of explanations have been a corner-stone of traditional psychology for a long time. The assumptions they rest on seem unquestionable. Our search for causes in past events has led us to focus primarily on the period of early childhood. We talk of the pre-school period as a person's 'formative years', the time when forces both psychological and environmental mould the person into the basic shape they will carry for the rest of their lives. Until relatively recently the field of developmental psychology referred exclusively to childhood, and particularly to early childhood. This preoccupation with childhood is a reflection of a more general notion of development which, in our culture at least, we all carry around with us. As a diagram, it would look something like this:

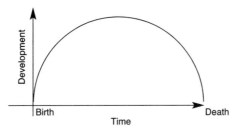

In childhood, we are progressing in our development. Change is the order of the day. In adulthood, our personalities having been formed by childhood experiences, development ceases and the rest of life is a period of 'negative development' characterised by the inevitable losses of old age – losses of mental agility, physical abilities, memory deficits and so on. As we pointed out earlier in this chapter, a brief reflection on our adult lives is at odds with this conception. If our subjective convictions that as adults we have undergone or are undergoing great changes or developments are not to be dismissed as illusions, any psychological theory of development has to take this into account.

Furthermore, this 'formative' model we are so used to does not cope well with a great deal of research evidence regarding the psychological effects of events in childhood. For example, it is true that deprivations of one sort or another appear to be related, in some children, to behavioural and emotional disturbances in adolescence and adulthood. However, by no means *all* children who have a deprived early life suffer problems later. And children who get off to a bad start in life, if given the opportunity for more positive experiences later, will often show dramatic improvements. The picture is also complicated by the fact that children whose early lives are dogged by trauma, through family disruption, conflict or poverty, often, through these social circumstances, *continue* to have a poor quality of life. In our search for causes of later psychological problems, we tend to ignore this and look for 'causes' in the 'formative years', in line with our implicit model of development.

So, appealing though this model is, it is not particularly good at accommodating either the research evidence or our own subjective experience.

Sense-making as 'Narrative'

Another weakness with this view of things is that, looking prospectively rather than retrospectively, it is much harder to make predictions about what events in a person's life will have a lasting impact upon him or her. Out of our vast range of experience, how is it that some events are 'formative' and others are not? And why do we remember some parts of our past and not others? Children and their parents constantly amaze each other by recalling 'insignificant' events or failing to recall 'significant' ones from their memories. The key, we feel, to these questions lies in the organising, sense-making propensity of human beings we talked of earlier.

When we look back over our lives, we struggle to make sense of past and present by fitting them together into some kind of historical account – a 'story' in fact. It is usually a story with a beginning, a middle and an end, bound together by a temporal theme – 'this happened, so that happened, and now I am like this' (see Gergen and Gergen, 1984; Salmon, 1985). This propensity to make sense of our experience by giving it a story-line can be seen when we look at our dreams. How we struggle to make something coherent from a chaotic muddle of unrelated and impossible occurrences! In answer to the question 'What did you dream last night?', we assemble the images and feelings into some kind of order that makes it possible to tell a story around them.

Where traditional psychology falls down is in missing the essential element in this process, and that is the active, constructive aspect of the endeavour. Just as we are actively constructing our visual perceptions, we also take an active, constructive stance to our perceptions of events and experiences. We construct a story around them that makes sense to us by a kind of selective attention. This is why we can come to feel that our memory is no good, or that we can't remember accurately, when our version of events fails to resemble that of other involved individuals. The model of memory we commonly adopt is one where all the events of our past are recorded and saved in some mental filing cabinet. Theoretically, any event can be recalled from a memory like this if you know where to look, Or perhaps we see memory as roll of film, constantly recording our experiences and storing them until needed. All we then have to do is rewind the film to the appropriate point and replay the event for accurate recall. This view of memory is apparent when we look at the controversy over the use of hypnosis in gathering eye-witness testimony. We see the hypnotist as a special kind of projectionist who can make the film rewind and replay in this manner. Research in this field, however, has demonstrated only too clearly that material gathered in this way is as much constructed as recalled, and that in this respect hypnotic memory operates in essentially the same way as memory in our usual, waking consciousness.

The constructive nature of memory explains why two people never remember the same aspects of the same event. Not only do we selectively perceive (i.e. we focus down upon what seems to us, through the nature of construing, the essential features), but in remembering the event we are constructing out of these features a story which makes sense to us in terms of our construal of the world, the perspective we bring to bear on it. So when we look back over our lives, we don't see it all in fine detail, or necessarily in chronological order. We see different episodes fitting together to make a story - 'the story of my life'. This is why it is a nonsense to talk of events having formative influences on people in any straightforward causative way. Rather, it is the meaning that is perceived in that event, the significance it has for our construal of our world, which has import for us.

What we are *not* saying, however, is that whatever your circumstances, life is what you make it. While it is our view that it is always the sense a person *makes* of an event, and not the event itself, which carries influence, it would be wrong to imply that all people have equal opportunities to improve their lives. Class, race, gender, unemployment, poverty and so on all impose real limitations on the freedom of individuals to reconstrue their life-story effectively.

Nor are we trying to imply that our subjective conviction that our past has great significance for our present (and our future) is no more than an illusion, only that this does not happen in a simple causative way. We carry around our past with us in our construing. To use the analogy of story writing, a person may have written' Chapters 1-6 of their life story in a tragic tone. How can they then envisage a happy ending? The value of a constructive alternativist view here is that, first, it is a more facilitative view of humanity than psychologies which see a person's nature as formed by experience and therefore more or less fixed for all time. And second, since we do not hold that we are 'formed' by our past experience, it is possible (though perhaps very difficult) for us to rewrite our history in order to envisage a better future.

Chapter 10
Why Have You Changed?

There is a rather condemnatory tone in the feel of this question. It is not a question that simply asks for an explanation, but one which also in some way implies blame - rather as we might ask a child why they had pulled the ears off their teddy bear. It seems to us that the issue of personal change is a value-laden one it is imbued with notions of what people *ought* or *ought not* to do.

Although we may be more accustomed to looking at change, in a positive way when we are considering children or adolescents ('How you've grown since I last saw you!'; 'She's blossomed into a woman in this past year!'), the way in which we talk about change in adulthood often has a more negative, disapproving and bewildered feel. We say 'You're not the man I married', or 'I just don't know you any more'. It's as if, in noting change in people we know, especially those who are important to us, this is an unwelcome state of affairs. It almost feels as if some unspoken gentleman's agreement has been broken; as if a bargain was struck in the early days of the relationship that we could always count on each other reliably to be the same person.

Predictability in our environment, including our social world, is undoubtedly important to us, and we make considerable efforts to structure our perceptions of the world such that, given any situation, we can quickly pick out of our behavioural experience an approximately appropriate action. We roughly classify events and people along the lines of 'If A, then B', giving us a rule of thumb for anticipating events. Without such devices our lives would be hopelessly chaotic - each event would be completely new and unique, and would have to be analysed afresh. Past experience would be no guide to future action. But useful as such a strategy is, it brings us problems in its wake. One of these problems, that of 'stereotyping', has been the focus of much interest from psychologists. When we use a stereotype, we attend to only a small amount of information about a person, such as their sex, age or race, and infer a whole range of other things about that individual on the basis of what we believe about that *group* of people.

Psychologists are not unaware that problems are entailed in our attempts to make our world, particularly our social world, a more or less predictable place to live in. But another problem which stems from this human characteristic is the conception of personality which it invites and, consequently, how we think about personal change.

The psychology, both academic and lay, through which we perceive people, offers us a world populated by individuals who 'have' differing amounts of assorted personality traits, with which we can expect to be able to predict their behaviour. We have already criticised this notion of personality, but the point here is that the allure of such a model is in the possibilities it seems to offer us to satisfy our desire to make the world predictable.

By deciding, once and for all, that Joe is a basically kind-hearted man, the tenor of our interaction with him, the part we envisage ourselves playing with respect to him, seems easy to work out. If Joe were a kind-hearted man one day, and a hard man the next, we would be at a loss how to expect an interaction with him. So we have a certain vested interest in a *static* notion of personality. If people stay more or less the same throughout their lives, we can be fairly sure of never (or hardly ever) feeling threatened or bewildered by their actions.

This 'static' view of personality has for a long time been at the root of how psychologists have thought about human development. As we saw in the last chapter, we imagine that the only significant changes in life occur in childhood – we have an image of the child as being 'formed' into the adult of their future life. Childhood is a journey, and adulthood is arrival at your destination. This notion of development sees adulthood as a kind of plateau – a huge expanse of time in which nothing much happens developmentally, apart from the milestones of marriage, parenthood, grandparenthood and retirement.

A small amount of personal reflection on this will reveal that it is nonsense. If we look back on our lives so far, we can usually point to at least one event or change in circumstances in our adult lives which, it seems to us at least, has had a major impact on us, either in the direction our life has taken or in the way in which it has made us see ourselves and those around us. While the importance of childhood experience should not be belittled, we need to take on board a dynamic model of adulthood in order to make sense of our personal experience.

However, simply acknowledging that change can and does take place throughout life is still not the whole story. And this is shown by our reaction to change. The question 'Why have you changed?', as well as being an admonition for a 'contract' broken, points to our assumption that the change must have been caused by something. We seek refuge in a model of humankind which sees people as inert lumps of matter being shaped and moulded by their environment. 'What *made* this happen?' we ask – our thinking is so firmly embedded in the notion of causality as an explanation for events, both physical and psychological, that we do not see that the question need not be asked in that way.

When we approach the issue of change from a personal construct standpoint, the question 'Why have you changed?' undergoes a complete reversal. A personal construct approach would not be affronted by change, or seek to find causal explanations of it, but rather starts from the *assumption* of change. Rather than ask 'Why have you changed?', change is assumed to be an inescapable part of being human, so that a person in whom *no* change was occurring would require an explanation.

Kelly's model of 'person as scientist' has each of us perpetually engaged in testing out our (often unarticulated) theories about our world and its inhabitants. Just as the scientist must make adjustments in a theory in order to accommodate new experimental findings, so are we all engaged in a continual process of matching our experience against our theory, as we work towards a more and more useful way of construing the world. This is not something we are *caused* to do by external events, but resides in the very nature of being human. Like the scientist, our adjusted theories lead us into new and different experiments – our personal constructs are formed out of our experience, which in turn leads to an adjustment of our constructs so that they can encompass ever widening categories of experience. We can see this process in operation when we look back to a time in our youth when things seemed much more 'black or white' than they do now. What has happened here? Our rough and ready 'black or white'-type constructs were rules of thumb which we gradually found to be inadequate for dealing with our experiences. Subtle changes and subdivision became necessary for us to make sense of life.

We may once have felt that people could pretty easily be categorised according to a 'moral versus immoral' dimension, based on what we saw of their behaviour or heard of their views. For example, 'People who fail to care for their elderly relatives are immoral' might have been our guiding theory. But in testing this theory, we soon come up against cases where people whom we have every reason to see as 'moral' in all other respects seem to be reluctant to care for an elderly relative. If we are to make any sense of this, we must allow our construct of morality–immorality to change in a way that will allow it to accommodate this new experience. Maybe we shall settle for a dimension which sees people in terms of those who do or don't 'have their whole family's welfare at heart'. This construct itself will change in the light of yet more experience.

The refusal to allow experience to tamper with our constructs gives us a false sense of security – we may feel safe in having pigeon holed the world, but the price we pay in the end is that many of the things people do will be inexplicable to us, just like the scientist who has developed a theory to explain some physical event, and becomes so attached to it that new and contradictory evidence is ignored or explained away.

Our experience does not only continually modify our construal of the world. Because we as humans have the capacity for self-reflection, we include our 'self' in the vast array of objects and events that we have experience of. Thus we construe ourselves too, and likewise this construing is a continuous process, necessarily leading to changes in the way we see ourselves.

Sometimes, like the scientist who shields his eyes from contradictory evidence, we suspect that our view of ourselves doesn't fit in with the evidence, but we may resist changing our construal of our self because it seems to us to lead to an unknown country where we just wouldn't know what to do – at least hanging on to our old view of ourself gives us *some* sort of recipe for action, no matter how inadequate!

But changes in the circumstances of our lives can often bring with them such a mountain of contradictory evidence that the old theory just has to be ditched so that within a relatively short period of time completely new constructs of oneself can emerge.

Joyce was an intelligent and hard-working young woman who had been to university and gained a degree. Although her friends and her colleagues in the solicitor's firm where she had recently come to work chose words such as 'bright', 'efficient' and 'good company' to describe her, she herself felt that this was an illusion she had promoted to cover up for her dullness, lack of intellect and shoddy work. When work went badly, she was confirmed in this view ('I'm just no good at my job'), but when work went well she refused to accept this as contradictory evidence for her self-theory ('It's just luck – no one but me knows how close I came to making a mess of it'). The pay-off of Joyce's self-theory was that she didn't have to have high expectations of herself, and therefore failure wasn't a threat. And up till this point in her life she had found it adequate in her dealings with the world – she didn't feel particularly happy about herself, but at least she knew where she was with this theory. Those who were closest to her had got used to her view of herself and adapted themselves to it, reassuring her and comforting her in her anxieties and never expecting her to make bold decisions.

But now the theory was beginning to make her miserable. She desperately wanted to be good at her job, but her self-theory wouldn't allow her to accept the evidence that she was good at her job, intelligent, well organised and pleasurable company. As she swept away each new piece of evidence, she concluded that she 'had to try harder'. Thus she climbed upon a treadmill of demanding more and more from herself, only to dismiss the fruits of her efforts as 'luck'.

The insight that it was her *construal* of herself that was her problem, not any inherent inadequacies, was the start of a new phase in her life. She gradually came to accept a less damaging self-construal and gained more and more pleasure from her new-found sense of achievement and self-worth.

But the story does not end here. For simultaneously life at home became rather more difficult for Joyce. She had been married to her husband, Richard, for ten years. Joyce had always depended on Richard for comfort in her anxieties and had looked to her marriage as a source of support against the threats of the outside world. For his part, Richard found it easy to be 'the strong one'. He was used to his wife's lack of self-confidence, and while he always offered her gentle encouragement, was always mindful of her need for him to be there if things got too much. He had, in fact, encouraged her to take on her job, after the usual years of home-making and child-rearing. They needed the extra money for their growing family, and it was clear to him that looking after a family was not always going to be enough for Joyce. He felt that the interest of a job would benefit her and, if she was enjoying her life more, this was bound to benefit the family as a whole. But what Richard had not anticipated was the change in Joyce's self-image which success in her job had given her, and the implication that this had for their relationship.

Joyce's new-found confidence in herself, and her sense of confidence, which she was deriving from her new perspective on her working life, was echoing throughout all spheres of her life. She was more self-assured generally, and more ready to credit herself with the fruits of her efforts. Minor challenges soon became tinged with pleasurable anticipation of success, rather than the threat of imminent failure. Although her attachment to Richard had not changed, she did not need him in quite the same way as before. She no longer felt she needed to depend upon *his* strength, as she saw herself as stronger and more competent than she had previously. She no longer needed to take refuge in his protection against the outside world, which was now rather more 'challenging' than 'threatening'.

Though Richard still loved his wife, he was confused and bewildered by the situation in which he found himself. The whole basis of his marriage, the unspoken rules by which they had interacted for ten years, no longer seemed to apply. He felt betrayed and could no longer make sense of his relationship with Joyce. He had expected going out to work to be a positive experience for her, and one which would make her life more interesting. But *why had she changed?*

Richard's reaction is familiar to us when we look at events where we have failed to envisage or anticipate the changes they would bring in their wake. This is partly due to our 'static' view of humankind, and to the negative value we typically place on personal change.

If we were instead to view personal change as something highly desirable, something to be expected and anticipated, perhaps we would not feel so betrayed when it happens. Kelly said 'man is a form of motion' – this means that the fundamental nature of human beings is to be constantly in a state of flux. Taking this view of humankind as our starting point, we can adopt a more enabling attitude towards those around us. We can begin to look for and anticipate change in them and in ourselves and even to consider that we ourselves are in the driving seat and can take responsibility for the direction our change takes. Such an attitude in psychology would represent real progress.

Part III
Reconstruing Illness

This section has in common with Part I an emphasis upon reconstruing common problems. What we are offering here is a primarily psychological construction of what are usually seen as physical, biological problems. These usual perspectives are 'reductionist' models, that is, they attempt to reduce a problem to lower levels of explanation. If we take a PCP view, we can see these kinds of explanations as existing among a range of alternative constructions, and the task then becomes one of identifying the construction or framework which is most useful to us in understanding the problem we are studying. We argue here that a psychological construal of common problems such as neurosis, anxiety, addiction and even pain can often be more fruitful than traditional biomedical approaches.

A second important theme throughout this section is the role that meaning plays in such problems. Kelly firmly believed that it is not events themselves which influence or mould people, torment or terrify them, or make them deliriously happy – it is the meaning with which these events are invested by the individual which is the potent ingredient.

Chapter 11 provides a short history of mental illness, showing that the categories we use for describing such problems have certainly been invented rather than discovered. We go on to suggest, by way of a case study, that the meaning underlying neurotic symptoms is a better starting point for therapy than the symptoms themselves. We have this much in common with the psychoanalysts, though we depart from them at the point where they begin searching for these meanings in the client's early life. PCP exhorts us to listen out for the meanings the people themselves seem to find in their experiences, and not to impose our own interpretations.

In Chapter 12 we continue to look at anxiety-provoking situations from the point of view of the meaning they hold for the individual. We can now begin to appreciate why people differ so greatly in the kinds of things they worry about.

The final two chapters put forward psychological constructions of what have come to be seen as largely physiological problems – pain and addiction. Our aim is to contrast traditional biomedical, reductionist models with a PCP approach which acknowledges the role of meaning in such problems. Chapter 13 also looks at the way that cartesian dualism has influenced thinking about pain. Dualism refers to the idea, originated by René Descartes, that human beings comprise two separate but interdependent realms of experience – the physical (body) and the mental (mind), and we argue that in many instances such a view of human experience gives rise to as many problems as it solves.

Chapter 11
Am I a Neurotic?

'Neurotic' is a term which, though a relatively recent acquisition to the language of mental disorders, has passed quickly into common usage. It is not unusual to hear someone respond to anxiety in others or in themselves with comments like 'Oh, you're just being neurotic about this', or 'I know I'm a bit neurotic really'.

As with the terms 'intravert' and 'extrovert', the term neurotic' is probably not being used in its originally intended sense. But, as in the case of these other psychological terms, it has come to have specific implications for people. We readily accept the idea that some people have a neurotic personality, which explains how they behave, or are 'suffering from' a neurosis, i.e. that they have an illness (in fact the concept of neurosis originated within medicine).

In this chapter, we shall look at the history of neurosis and then argue two points:

1. That although it refers to real problems it offers only an inexact description and virtually no explanation of them.
2. That while it can be sensible to describe psychological processes as neurotic, it makes no sense whatever to apply the term to people.

First, then, the history and development of the term 'neurosis'. Psychoses, neuroses and personality disorders are seen by the medical profession as the major subdivisions of the superordinate concept of mental illness. 'Mental illness' is one of those constructions that we are likely to accept as a fact of life or discovery, rather than an invention. The power, prestige and influence of the medical profession can blind us to alternative constructions of the phenomena that constitute mental illness. We should remember, however, that the framework of illness is one that has been applied within only the past 100 years to problems that people have always had. Although you can occasionally hear the odd psychiatrist declare that Jesus and Joan of Arc were schizophrenics or

Richard the Lionheart was really a psychopath, these people were not regarded as such in their own times. In Britain the concept of lunacy predated mental illness, and lunatics were largely carved out of a larger public nuisance group. A series of parliamentary acts legislated the insane into existence and prescribed how they should be disposed of or treated. Whereas criminals were seen as responsible for their crimes and punished, and the poor and vagrants were set to work in workhouses, lunatics were confined in asylums. These concepts, then, were essentially legal, but with the rise of the medical profession, lunatics were increasingly seen as being ill. In early Victorian times, doctors had not had much success in either explaining or treating (far less curing) physical illness. Even in the American Civil War (1861–1865) more soldiers died from infected wounds and disease than on the battlefield. The advent of microscopy and the discovery of micro-organisms rendered many diseases understandable, if not yet treatable, in medical terms. Diagnosis sought first to identify separate diseases with identifiable signs and symptoms, then to discover the cause or aetiology. This, it was hoped, would lead to ways of both preventing and treating the illness. When it was found that many asylum inmates suffering from so-called general paralysis of the insane (GPI) were in fact suffering from tertiary syphilis, there was optimism that in time other forms of insanity could be traced to organic causes and regarded as mental illnesses. Incidentally, the story of GPI also provided good ammunition for those moralists who thought that sexual licence in its various manifestations provided an explanation for mental illness generally.

Now the history of lunacy is largely the history of psychoses, as opposed to neuroses. Today, the psychoses (e.g. senile and presenile dementia, the schizophrenias) are seen as the more severe and catastrophic mental illnesses, and it is most likely that it was those people who would now be termed 'psychotic' who mainly populated the county asylums around the year 1900. Psychotic patients are said to lack insight into their complaint, to have lost contact with reality and to have suffered global and severe disintegration of the personality. The neuroses, by contrast, are seen as less disabling and severe. In these complaints (e.g. phobias, obsessions, hysteria) the patient preserves insight and does not lose contact with reality; they 'know' there's nothing to be afraid of in going out, and that there is no real need to cheek the gas taps for the seventh time, or wash their hands three times after visiting the lavatory, but this doesn't stop them being afraid and actually washing or checking – or at least wanting to wash or check. While the psychotic's experience is said to be *qualitatively* different from normal experience, the neurotic's is seen as being only *quantitatively* different. So (for most of the time, at least!) most of us are not disoriented in time or place, and we have not forgotten our names or who we are. But all of us can feel anxious or depressed, or obsessed with something or someone. This is perhaps why people don't ask 'Am I a psychotic?', (although many worry about 'going mad'), whereas 'Am I a neurotic?' is frequently felt, if not asked, with an uncomfortable mixture of anxiety and shame.

How is it, then, that these feelings and processes that we all know at first hand have come to be seen as evidence of illness? The history of neurosis dates back to the late nineteenth century, and began on the continent, with physicians like Jean-Martin Charcot. The concept was developed and elaborated within the tradition of psychoanalysis. 'Psychoanalysis' is a term that is often misused and misunderstood: it is properly used to refer to both a psychological theory of human development and a psychotherapeutic treatment based on the works of Freud. Although Freud's ideas were initially treated with scorn and derision, many of them have been incorporated (albeit in different forms) in the conventional psychiatry of western Europe and particularly in the USA. Like Charcot before him, Freud was originally concerned with the problem of hysteria (see Breuer and Freud, 1894). This was the diagnosis given to those cases where the patient presented with a complaint that appeared to be physical (e.g. a pain or a paralysis) but on investigation was revealed to have no organic basis, no physical cause. Now doctors then, as now, did not take kindly to what they saw as counterfeit complaints, which can be seen as wasting the doctor's time and effort. Freud's great contribution was to 'analyse' the complaint in terms of the patient's (unconscious) wishes and forces (see 'Am I Imagining This Pain?' Chapter 13). In so doing he preserved the status of illness that the patient had sought, and declared hysterias a proper currency for physicians to deal in. The humanitarian thrust of psychiatry in seeking illness labels for its patients must not be underestimated; even so, there are dangers lurking in the wake of this pathologising of human misery and unhappiness. The principal one is that behaviour that society disapproves of can be dismissed as merely neurotic, and the diagnosis of 'neurotic' can become a despised label, and a very sticky one at that – one that can overshadow valid reasons that people have for acting in the way they do. Political dissidents and radicals, for example, can be safely brushed aside – 'Oh there's something wrong with her...', He's not all there', we say. It is no mistake that psychiatric language changes its meaning as it enters everyday parlance. 'Hysteric', 'psychopath', 'neurotic' are frequently terms of abuse. To say someone is 'obsessed', is to hint at a lack of rationality. It is interesting to note that 'moron', 'cretin' and 'idiot' all started life as medical terms, each referring to discrete bands of IQ. Yet these terms now have exclusively pejorative meanings. This perhaps accounts for the shame and guilt we face when we wonder whether we are neurotic. Sympathy may and should accompany the sick role, but we are aware of the high price we may well pay for it.

This history is important, since it makes clear that when we talk of neurosis, we are dealing with a particular construction of truth, not the raw truth itself. PCP holds that this is always so – events can be construed in a number of ways. The question is: is it a helpful construction?', i.e. does it explain those phenomena called neurotic, and does it help us to change them?

We have noted that the whole point of diagnosis is to pinpoint the cause and treatment of a complaint. The first stage is to describe the complaint and separate it from others – to categorise. The second is to link each disease, each category, with a particular aetiology, hopefully with helpful implications. In the case of neuroses, psychiatric diagnosis has never progressed beyond the first classification stage. The different neuroses – anxieties, phobias, depressions, obsessions, compulsions, hysterias - remain crude descriptions of how people think, feel and act in ways that are a problem to them. Modern psychiatrists no longer adhere to simple disease models and do not expect to find organic or physical aetiologies of the neuroses. Instead these problems are seen as being psychogenic in origin. This means that it is the individual's experience, perhaps in early life, that holds the key to their neuroses. It is here that psychiatry turns to a mishmash of (usually outdated) psychological theories such as early psychoanalysis or the conditioning theories of the early behaviourists. However, any attempt to link discrete neuroses to particular events in a personal history were doomed. Study after study has shown that assigning diagnoses to discrete separate illness categories is hopelessly unreliable: diagnosticians can only rarely agree on who has what illness. This is surely because neurotic complaints do not fall neatly into categories. It is nigh-on impossible to distinguish between the obsessional, the depressive, the hysteric and the so-called normal state. The medical construction simply does not fit the facts.

Yet people *do* suffer from 'neurotic' miseries, sometimes to the extent that their lives are severely impaired. People feel unreasonably scared of fainting, going out, being sick, eating in public. People feel convinced that something nameless and dreadful is going to happen, and spend all their energies guarding against it in idiosyncratic rituals, washing, checking and praying. But the construct 'neurotic versus healthy' is a nonsense, because all the so-called healthy people have neurotic problems as well. Maybe not so many problems, maybe not as severe, but there is no definition of mental health that holds water. They vary from time to time and from place to place. There are strong arguments that all the best work is done by obsessionals, wars could not be won without psychopaths, and anyone who doesn't get depressed is just not in contact with the realities of the world.

However, we would argue that although you cannot divide people into the neurotic and the healthy (still less into various different types of neurotic), there is a useful distinction to be made between common unhappiness and neurotic misery (a distinction originally made by Freud). Perhaps 'distinction' is the wrong word to use here; rather one fades into the other – we are dealing with a continuum rather than separate categories. It is very hard indeed to say when grief becomes depression, when reasonable care becomes obsessional, and when a fear becomes a phobia. But we recognise excesses of emotion or behaviour that cost us dear, that we would like dealt with. It matters not whether our complaints are normal, whether someone else could put up with them. There is no standard of mental health against which we can calibrate ourselves. Every survey shows that for every person seeking psychiatric treatment there are several with similar problems who do not.

Storr (1979) suggests that what distinguishes those who seek treatment from those who don't is not a particular degree of psychopathology, but how demoralised people are in the face of it. Here we return to the guilt that often accompanies the question 'Am I neurotic?'. We feel we must apologise for our irrationality: 'I know it's stupid but....' This sense of conflict reflects what psychiatrists see as the preservation of insight. It also speaks of the experience of being driven, not being the captain of your own ship. Kovel (1976) terms this a lack of inner freedom, and it is identified by various psychological theorists as central to the neurotic state.

So we have said that you cannot categorise people as neurotic, and neurotic problems cannot be characterised by reference to particular symptoms. However, people frequently feel in conflict, and a mystery to themselves. We live in a culture which unhelpfully divides psychological processes into thoughts and feelings, and we are not encouraged to develop a language of feelings to articulate their meanings. They tend to be dismissed as senseless, but they can be difficult to ignore. Psychological therapies generally explore these unelaborated meanings and are helpful when people feel overwhelmed and mystified by their own psychology.

Right across the spectrum of psychological theories, there seems to be agreement that anxiety is a necessary ingredient in a neurotic problem. This provides a good example of a difference between a psychiatric (medical) and a psychological approach to problems. Kelly proposed that anxiety is a sign that we are construing in unknown areas, are confronted with events we can't yet make sense of or deal with. Consequently it is not something to be merely tranquillised and damped down. It may be advisable to tackle the anxiety in such a way, but this must not blind us to what it signals: events that must be confronted.

Kath felt that she was an over-sensitive, neurotic woman. Things were worst when she had to eat in the company of others. She had lived with the problem since adolescence, but a new man in her life, and the prospect of visiting more restaurants, had brought the issue to a head. Although she thought of her complaint as a fear of eating in public, the therapist was struck by her intense embarrassment at the problem. She thought that maybe her relatives and best friend guessed that she had this difficulty, but certainly her new man friend did not. It is not uncommon that people feel they are an open book to others when they are not. They imagine that other people are as acutely aware of their problem as they are themselves, and feel exposed, shamed and degraded. And this is as much a problem as what they identify as 'the problem' itself. In Kath's case, her worry about being seen while eating turned out to be part of a general issue of feeling odd, and bizarre, in the eyes of others. Her secret shame and embarrassment at the problem nourished these beliefs and reinforced the eating problem.

A PCP approach highlights what her anxieties are about. It is not concerned with just getting rid of them. Kath had a long-established theory that people find her peculiar, abnormal. Her solution had been to restrict her social circle to those she was fairly certain of. Now she was no longer avoiding people and consequently was having to construe new events. What did that look mean? And that sideways glance? Anxiety and self-doubt inevitably accompanied her new experimentation. She needed and profited from help. We could translate this into psychiatrese and call the problem neurotic, but nowadays, when people confuse this with a term of abuse, it is a label best avoided. Seeing her as a neurotic who has an illness misleadingly envelops us in such language as 'treatment' and 'cure'. We come to see anxiety as a problem in itself that simply needs quietening down or tranquillising. While it may need attention in its own right, PCP insists that we don't think of panic and anxiety as like an accident of spilt adrenaline: it is *about* something, it makes psychological sense and unless this is appreciated and dealt with, it will recur.

In personal construct therapy the subject is not a patient, a passive recipient of treatment, but resembles a research student who has his or her own projects, theories and hypotheses ('person-as-scientist'). The therapist is something of a research supervisor, and therapy itself is best seen as an educational exercise. When you start a piece of research, you normally have an area of interest, some questions about it, and perhaps some theories as to why things happen as they do. In the early stages of supervision your supervisor would try to understand your interest and help you sharpen up your ideas and questions, to get them into some form where you can expect some answers. This answering would be the 'meat' of the project. It might involve experiments, observation, library searching or some other form of investigation. Drawing some conclusions should complete the cycle. Anyone who has been through the process will testify that it's never easy (apparent brilliance is usually 5% inspiration and 95% perspiration), and the questions you end up with are rarely the ones you started out with! Certainly your initial ideas and framing of questions look over-simplified. This process corresponds exactly to therapy: you can do it on your own or with friends, but larger projects often require a supervisor. However, *your* project always remains your project. You know most about it, you retain control – you can ditch it if you want to. The supervisor's expertise is in helping you to frame your questions, broaden your scope, elaborate your interests. The supervisor should help you develop appropriate methods of investigation and help you to draw reasonable conclusions. We shall return to this 'research' metaphor in our final chapter on personal change, as we feel it to be a particularly appropriate way conceptualising personal construct therapy.

Kath's initial question was 'How do I get rid of this nervousness?'. Therapy involved elaborating this question, coming at it from a different direction. What was the anxiety about? It seemed likely that it was about Kath's beliefs/feelings about herself. Note that this is not an interpretation; it is a proposition. An interpreter tells you what things mean; a research scientist says 'Have you thought of this...?' and suggests possibilities rather than tells you truths about yourself. The investigation phase of the research/therapy must involve some sort of venture – it cannot be wholly an armchair exercise. Trying things out, testing the water – perhaps first with the therapist, through relatively safe situations before trying the big experiments (say eating in restaurants with a large group of acquaintances). The point of the investigation is to help answer the questions, for example 'Well, am I odd? Do people find me disgusting?' etc.

Does therapy work – is it effective? Do research projects work? Is conversation effective? Don Bannister considered this one of the silliest questions (Bannister, 1983). Certainly no simple measures of effectiveness can be devised. You might go into therapy to change your sexuality but come out happy to live with it. You might seek help because you are depressed and come to realise that you've good reason to be. But both good education and good therapy involve the elaboration of possibilities, the empowering of people.

Maybe you could say we're all neurotic from time to time; perhaps some more so than others. However, 'neurotic' is, in the end, one of those labels that conceals more than it reveals. In Kelly's terms, it is used pre-emptively. This means that we tend to think 'this person is a neurotic, *and nothing but a neurotic*'. This 'nothing but...' thinking means that we miss other things about the person – everything they do is a result of their neuroticism. This is why Kelly (1955) introduced the notion of 'transitive diagnosis' to replace psychiatric diagnosis. Transitive diagnosis focuses not on categorising, but on looking for avenues of psychological movement that the person may capitalise on. As Winter (2003) emphasises, the 'neurotic' process is not qualitatively different from so-called healthy functioning. So, for example, everyone has moments of loose construing, in which their functioning is vague and ill defined. Similarly, each of us also has times when we construe tightly, making well-defined and exact moves and predictions. In fact, Kelly believed that cycling between loose and tight construing was what constitutes creativity. But when someone does either exclusively, they are likely to exhibit some form of psychological distress and disorder – they might be seen as either schizophrenic or obsessional, for example. Winter suggests that we should therefore think not so much of psychological disorders like neurosis as of psychological imbalances. The advantage of this is pragmatic: we might then be able to think about corrective strategies the client may use in our transitive diagnosis.

In the next chapter we continue to explore anxiety from a PCP perspective. We ask why it is that different people find different things anxiety provoking, or why two people who are apparently afraid of the same thing cannot be assumed to have equivalent anxieties or problems.

Chapter 12
Why Worry?

How often are we asked this, when we are anxious about some improbable event? 'Worrying never did any good ' we are told – and we have to agree. The problem is that the advice doesn't seem to help us, we worry despite the knowledge that it's useless, a waste of effort and resources, and feel all the more inadequate at our irrationality. This question and its entailed advice seems to assume that we can stop worrying by an act of will. Yet it does not seem to us that we have *chosen* to worry, although we are surrounded by people who seem to accept fate and get on with the business of living.

So why do we worry? We don't dispute that it is useless, and invariably even counterproductive, for two reasons: first, because it stops us getting any enjoyment out of the present, leading us instead to dwell on apocalyptic visions of the future; and second, because it is likely to hamstring us in the event of actual crisis, leading down the path of paralysis and indecision rather than that of effective action and damage limitation. Perhaps, we muse, there are born worriers. Many psychologists would agree with this, proposing that there are genetically endowed differences in our autonomic lability, a physiological function that underpins what they construe as emotions such as anxiety. But if this true, why do people worry about different things? One may be cruelly tormented by the possibility of a plane crash while another may be perfectly at ease in the air, only to be tortured by the possibilities of ill health. This attempt at a physiological explanation is one construction, an attempt to make sense of individual differences in manifest anxiety, but one that we contend is of limited value in understanding human misery.

A more profitable – and psychological – construal is to seek explanation in terms of an individual's outlook or construct system and the meaning they extract from the situations with which they are confronted. Certainly we shall not understand someone's anxiety by looking at the situations *per se* since, as we have seen, people are frightened by different things. Telling a child there is no reason to fear the dark, loud noises or a fly in the room, is unlikely to lead to a reduction in anxiety. Yet it is this blindness to personal meaning that leads the baffled observer, from his or her very different vantage point, to ask 'Why worry?' and to assert that worrying is useless – indeed a silly question and advice that is easy to give but impossible to follow.

The key, then, to appreciating worry is in understanding individual differences in construing. This, of course, is extremely difficult to do, since none of us ever sees a situation (or an event, in Kellian terminology) as it is: our perception is always coloured by our own construct system, the spectacles through which we attempt to apprehend reality. It is a platitude that no one knows whether we all perceive a basic element like the colour red in the same way. We can never see things through someone else's eyes, and any differences will be disguised through the labelling process which leads to everyone calling red by the same verbal label. A common language is necessary to enable communication, but it will sometimes conceal more than it reveals. It is a gross mistake to assume that two people faced with the same objective reality face the same subjective reality. If this is true with a simple colour how much more is it true in the case of nuclear war, a plane crash or a fatal illness? Within each individual's construct system, each of these events will be linked to a complicated network of consequences, meanings and images. There will certainly be some shared meaning between people – what Kelly calls commonality. But it is better not to assume this in our investigation of anxiety and threat, and instead expect individuality in construing.

How, then, can we approach this aspect of another's individuality, hampered as we are by our own taken-for-granted constructions? There is no substitute here for conversation talking, questioning and careful listening. This sounds too obvious at first, but in fact it is extraordinary how little people listen to one another in everyday life. Very often, what passes for conversation is competitive, talking, relating anecdotes, and attempting to impress others. These may all have their place in social life, along with various rituals of the 'How-are-you-very-well-thank-you' variety, but they are not to be confused with the sort of conversation where people try to understand each other. Nowadays there is a danger that we distil this off and reserve it for 'counsellors' – as though listening to other people requires some sort of professional skill.

> Mike was terrified by the prospect of nuclear war. You may say 'Well, who isn't?' or perhaps 'Well, there's no point in getting anxious, if it happens it happens there's nothing you can do about it!'. You may have many other reactions, but these were the two that he encountered most often, at least when he wasn't too embarrassed to admit his fear. Both are varieties of the 'Why worry?' response, of course. It was mainly a secret fear; he would spend hours listening to news broadcasts and, combing newspapers for evidence of his theory that nuclear

catastrophe was imminent. Other people noticed his gloom but did not know the reason for it. The reason why people didn't understand him was perhaps that nuclear war meant different things to him and them. They were not envisaging the same thing. Their image was one of immediate total annihilation – one minute they would be alive and the next dead. His nuclear war was one of slow, lingering death; burnt screaming children to whom he could offer no hope; starvation, sickness, cold and tears. Whether Mike or those around him have the more realistic assessment does not matter; the point is that they have different visions, inhabit different worlds when they talk of nuclear war. The reason Mike worries is that the shape of his nightmare fits too closely into his projection of nuclear catastrophe. The most productive questions become 'Why *this* theme, *this* nightmare?', 'Where else does he see echoes of it?', 'What led to his developing the theory...?'

Phyllis said she had a phobia of flying. It stopped her and her young family taking holidays abroad, and irritated her husband, who kept pointing out that there was no safer form of travel than an aircraft. Phyllis did not dispute this: it was not the issue that mattered. What terrified her was the thought of the power, speed and lack of control that jet travel entailed.

It is a mistake to assume that we know what aspect of a phobic situation is the active ingredient in any particular individual's fear. Indeed, our own fears may seem stupid and beyond the reach of reason to us. We have devoted a chapter to the issue of reason versus emotion, in which we propose that all feelings have some reasoning behind them. However, psycho-logic may be idiosyncratic and poorly articulated.

When we are unable to understand our own fears we need some way of elaborating and spelling out our reasons. If we can't do this in conversation with others we can try the next best thing: some sort of formalised conversation with ourselves.

Don Bannister, one of PCP's leading proponents, used to recommend a technique called 'McFall's Mystical Monitor' for helping people elaborate in this way.

1. You speak for 15 min into a tape recorder on, say, 'Why I'm scared of plane travel?'. The only rule is that you must keep talking: if you dry up you have to explain why you have.
2. You listen to the recording then rewind and erase it.
3. You repeat the exercise for a 30-min session.
4. Once more you erase the tape: you must be the only audience.

One of the revealing things about this exercise is how difficult it is to talk and say certain things since you're promised that there will be no other audience except yourself. One issue you have to address is who is the audience/monitor that you place in the role of listener? Once you have begun to speak more openly and 'freewheel' in the monologue you might be able to articulate areas of your construct system that have previously been pre-verbal and murky. Kellian psychology does not believe in a dynamic unconscious, where things are repressed and held out of consciousness because of their anxiety-provoking properties, but it does hold that some constructions are beneath our level of awareness. This might sometimes be because we would rather not look at them, but often it is because the constructions were formed before we were able to give verbal labels to them. Children learn to construe situations and people along some dimension such as 'safe-and-secure/unknown-and-worrying' before they can say why some situations belong to one end or other of the continuum. In adult life many agoraphobic people are unable to say why some situations are worrying or downright terrifying and others safe, yet they are in no doubt as to where situations belong on this dimension.

If the Mystical Monitor does not help them work out the nature of 'safe versus unsafe', some sort of pencil and paper exercise may. One could begin by taking a series of situations, some safe and some unsafe, and then comparing them to look for all the similarities and differences between them. This would be a type of repertory grid (see Part V), and its aim would be to expose a pattern of constructs that makes more clear the nature of 'safe–unsafe' for a particular person. In Phyllis's case, safety decreased: (1) when she was enclosed; (2) when she was in a crowd; (3) when she felt helpless; (4) when she couldn't get home quickly; (5) when she was unaccompanied by her husband. With the exception of condition (5), plane travel represented everything that was insecure to her.

Throughout this chapter we have used the terms 'anxiety' and 'threat' interchangeably. Kelly attempted finer discrimination between these terms, based on individuals' construing. We experience what he called anxiety when we are faced with events that we cannot map on to our construct system. These are the proverbial 'things that go bump in the night', and in general are the things we just can't explain in terms of our usual ways of construing – our construct system literally can't make sense of them.

'Threat' constitutes an altogether more serious problem, and it is the Kellian notion of threat that is perhaps most relevant in understanding an individual's persistent worries. We feel threatened when events rock the foundation stones of our construct system. The constructs which are superordinate for us are the ones that define the core of our identity, without which we would have little concept of ourselves as people. They are also the constructs which are fundamental to the way we make sense of our world, and we may trace back many of our subordinate constructs to this source, like tributaries of a great river. If *these* constructs are called into question by the results of our experiments with life, it is not surprising that we feel threatened. Our superordinate constructs are the linchpin that holds us together.

Most of us have a nightmare, a 'worst possible' scenario which we ponder with horror - 'If *that* should happen, I would fall apart...'. For each of us, our own personal nightmare scenario will in some way embody this 'falling apart', the removal of our linchpin. In George Orwell's *1984*, room 101 is used to break the resistance of even the toughest, since it is designed to contain his or her particular nightmare. In the case of the hero, the presence of rats brings about defeat and compliance that other tortures could not compete with because of the meaning they embodied for him.

Looked at in this way, we should not be surprised if, say, a person for whom 'being in control versus having no control' is a superordinate construct were terrified of air travel. We should certainly not think of this fear as irrational, or wonder at the inability to take heed of 'the facts' such as the relative safety of air versus car travel, etc.

Surely everyone has such a nightmare. At a safe distance, in the cinema or the chamber of horrors, they fascinate us. But if we sense a real probability of their happening we shall worry, whether or not it looks logical to others. What we have to try to do is understand the shape of the nightmare, and how it fits so well the situation that appears to terrify us.

Chapter 13
Am I Imagining This Pain?

People often visit their doctor with a pain that is worrying them, perhaps recurrent headaches, but in many cases the doctor can find nothing wrong with them. An immediate reaction might be a feeling of relief that there is 'nothing to worry about', but this may soon be followed by doubt and unease. After all, the pain certainly *felt* real enough, and since we believe that pain is nature's way of telling us that something is wrong with our body, we may be tempted to wonder if the doctor has overlooked some lurking pathology. EEGs and brain scans may confirm that there is no organic cause for the pain, yet we may remain unconvinced that there is nothing wrong.

This leaves us with a problem: if there is no physical cause for the pain, it cannot be real, cannot be said to exist in quite the same way as organically based pain. If it is not real, it must be unreal, or imagined. Pursuing this line of thought further, we reason that if the pain is not real, and we are imagining it, then our experience is out of touch with reality and we must be bordering on insanity. Perhaps 'imagining' pain is similar to 'imagining' voices or having visual hallucinations.

Clearly this is a ridiculous conclusion. We know that people who feel pain for which there is no organic cause are not insane. But how, then, can we make sense of their experience?

The heart of the problem, and the reason why 'Am I imagining this pain?' is a bad question, lies in three fundamental assumptions that we commonly make when thinking about and explaining our experience.

First of all, let us go back to a phrase that we used earlier – 'pain is nature's way of telling us that something is wrong with our body'. If we examine this statement we find that we are talking about 'us' and 'our body' as two separate entities. If 'us' does not refer to our bodies, perhaps it refers to our minds'. The assumption that 'we' (i.e. minds) in some way inhabit (but are separate from) our bodies is so fundamental to our thinking that we fail to notice it unless we take the trouble to scrutinise our language like this. And yet people have not always thought about themselves in this way. As we saw earlier, thinking of people as comprising a duality of parts, minds and bodies, is a relatively recent idea which gained currency after the writings of René Descartes (the idea is therefore known as 'Cartesian dualism' or simply 'dualism').

We can now see that the way in which we typically think about our experience, in this dualistic fashion, is a *construct* – that is, we divide up our experience into 'the mental' and 'the physical'. When looking at any aspect of our experience, a fundamental question we are always posing (though we are not perhaps aware of it) is 'Is this experience physical or mental?'. To come back to our example of the visit to the doctor, the issue for the GP is whether the pain has any organic cause and needs treatment. But doctors see countless cases of genuine pain that they cannot explain. In keeping with the dualistic notion just outlined, neurologists and psychiatrists have speculated that in some way 'mental' pain can be 'converted' into physical pain. The diagnosis of 'conversion hysteria' was devised to describe those pains and other physical symptoms that appear to be psychogenic – have their origins in psychological rather than physical factors. Such diagnoses are attempts to make sense of non-organic pain within the mind–body dualistic framework.

Like any other construct that we may hold in our repertoire, these categories are mutually exclusive; a pain thus cannot be both physical *and* mental. But also, like any construct, it should not be judged by its truth (i.e. by asking whether an event is in fact physical or mental), but by its usefulness. That is, does it help us to make sense of our experience? Obviously on many occasions looking at events as if they were either physical or mental can be useful in ordering our experience (it is certainly useful for the doctor), but in the case of pain it does not always lead us to helpful explanations.

Mind–body dualism is, then, the first assumption that underlies our thinking about pain, and we can see it as a construct. But a second assumption or construct closely associated with the 'mental–physical' one is 'real–imaginary'. If we must divide the world up into physical events and mental events we are invited to construe only physical events as real. The rest is imagination. This is how, having found that their pain has no physical basis, a person is led to the uncomfortable conclusion that 'it's all in the mind'. Furthermore, the term 'hysterical' is hardly likely to comfort, since it is one of the many psychiatric terms that have been adopted in everyday language as insults.

And, of course, the person is still left with the problem of what is causing the pain. When minds became viewed as entities separate from bodies, the realm of the mental also became a kind of parallel universe to the physical. The explanations that were commonly used to account for physical events became available to mental ones too. So just as we have physical illness, we talk of 'mental illness' and think of minds as becoming sick, being treated and cured, in much the same way as bodies. To see why this is a problem for explanations of pain we have to look again at the language in which we express ourselves, to find the third basic assumption. We have talked of physical 'causes' of pain – but the notion of causality is so fundamental to our thinking, that we take it for granted (we have already met this assumption in Chapter 9). But where have we borrowed it from? In the physical world, we have an abundance of events that are explained in terms of causality.' When I turn my car ignition key, my action triggers off a chain of events which causes a spark to ignite a mixture of fuel and air in the engine. Causality is in essence the world of the machine, a world of knock-on effects with inevitable outcomes. But we have taken the world of the machine into our bodies – we have adopted it as a metaphor, a model of our physical selves. The tendency for people to think of themselves generally in mechanical terms probably began in the mid-nineteenth century, which saw both the industrial revolution and the rise of medicine. With techniques like microscopy, scientists discovered previously invisible structures and organisms such as cells and bacteria. The explanations, or 'causes' of various previously mysterious illnesses, such as tuberculosis, were understood for the first time. But the notion of 'causes' is of course borrowed from the language of the machine, where every effect must have a cause, something that kicked it into action. The car does not drive away by itself, but does so at the end of a chain of events initiated by the driver. Further evidence of how we think mechanistically about ourselves shows in our language. We talk of 'having energy' and 'running out of ideas' in much the same way as machines have potential energy and run out of fuel.

Let us see how this mechanistic metaphor handles the dualistic notion of mind–body. The mind's relationship to the body is seen as being rather like that of a driver to a car. You can have mechanical faults and human error and various interactions between the two. Crashing the gears or slipping the clutch will eventually take its toll on the car in much the same way that bad diet, lack of exercise or smoking will on the body. It is easy to understand how a driver might feel insulted if he took his faulty car to a garage only to be told that there was nothing wrong with the car (except for normal wear and tear) and that any fault lay with the driver. Thus the first problem that arises with mechanistic notions of the mind–body relationship is one of blame and responsibility. Blame and responsibility are terms that may be applied to drivers, but not to cars. We cannot blame someone for the pain experienced due to a broken leg (though we might disapprove of their rock-climbing), but non-physical pain seems to raise uncomfortable questions of responsibility. A second problem is to do with causality. When we make the mental world a parallel form of the physical, we also imbue it with many of the same mechanistic properties. Thus, just as we seek causes for physical events, such as the notion of specific aetiology in illness, we seek them as explanations for mental ones too. 'If I'm not ill, what is causing these headaches?' But looking for explanations in terms of causes leads us into difficulties. A problem with mechanistic metaphors of humankind is how we explain our feeling that although things do happen to us, we also do things that we feel responsible for – what can be called our experience of agency and responsibility. Furthermore, once we stop looking for triggers for events (such as pain) and instead ask what the person is doing, an explanation becomes possible. Let us illustrate this with an example.

Alan experienced painful headaches. He was a socially confident and articulate person, but the pains dispirited him. He could not predict their occurrence: they represented an area of his life over which he had no control.

A close examination of the times and situations in which the pain occurred indeed showed that there was no person or place that was guaranteed to bring it on. It tended to occur more in the presence of challenging people, but it soon became clear that this was less to do with them than with his feelings under stress, of which they were likely to constitute one component. We can see here that although it is tempting to look for 'stimuli' that 'trigger' a 'response', an explanation in such terms would be shallow. Our understanding must be couched in terms of what Alan makes of things, rather than of what the things are actually like.

Alan was a capable man who found he could cope with things better than most people around him. In any group, he was the one who sorted everything out, and could be relied on to do the organising, the running about. He had developed sensitive antennae which he relied on to tell him what people wanted, which was important in both his social and business life. One lesson he had learned was 'If I don't cope, then nobody else will!'. It was as though he lived his life following rules like 'Always be strong' and 'Never rest; just keep going'.

What options are open to people when they are worn out, meet people that seem critical or difficult to please, or feel like crying?

Alan was encouraged to personify his headache and initiate a dialogue within, to interrogate it. The results indicated that the pain was his only way of expressing frustration, and what he saw as weakness. He needed encouragement to reconstrue his relationships and sense of responsibility towards others.

What we have been trying to show in this chapter is that when we attempt to construe events as *either* physical *or* mental (psychological) we tend to create mysteries for ourselves, such as a pain that is not 'real'. The physical versus psychological arguments are of course not limited to the issue of pain: psychologists and philosophers have long debated whether there is a mind or soul, a 'ghost in the machine' (dualism), or whether there is only a very sophisticated machine, i.e. that all events that we now feel compelled to label as psychological will eventually become explainable in physical terms, for example particular patterns of circuitry in the brain (reductionism). The problem is that dualism and reductionism have been cast as alternatives that we must choose between, yet they are both alike in that they see things in terms of the physical or the psychological; something is either one or it is the other. 'Cancer and broken limbs are physical, but dreams and imagination are psychological', the dualist says. 'No', replies the reductionist, 'during dreams and imagination there is electrical activity the in the brain that can be measured'.

We want to suggest a radical alternative to both dualism and reductionism, to propose that we abandon the physical versus psychological construct when it ceases to make sense of our experience for us. Phenomena do not come bearing labels such as physical and psychological – these are the tags that we give them to bring structure and order to our experience. So a thing in itself cannot be said to *be* physical or psychological. If we take an example like depression, this becomes clear. It makes no sense to ask whether depression is in fact a physical or a psychological phenomenon – we can identify symptoms which could carry both kinds of labels. But what we *can* do is to look at people from either a physical or a psychological *point of view*. Our guide should be: 'Which perspective, in any particular instance, will be most helpful in making sense of the phenomenon?'. The important thing about seeing the physical and the psychological as perspectives or constructions rather than as real properties of events is that they are not then mutually exclusive.

The question is not 'What is pain really?' but 'What perspective is most helpful in this instance?'. We are accustomed to viewing pain physically, and the physical construction is so often validated that we are likely to think of pain as a physical thing rather than as something that can often be usefully construed physically. To begin to construe pain psychologically we must certainly avoid questions about the mechanisms connecting mind and body – they are predicated on the dualist assumptions which we have described but do not accept. The issue of real versus imaginary pain thus also becomes obsolete; we can then ask 'What is being communicated by this pain, or expressed through it: *what does it mean?*'.

Chapter 14
Am I an Addict?

The concept of addiction is one which is familiar to us these days. We see people's lives being ruined by addiction to drugs or alcohol, and there seems little reason to argue with the usual explanation: some substances, when taken regularly, eventually create a state of biological dependency in the body. This means that, in time, a person's body becomes accustomed to the substance, physiological changes occur, and it then becomes impossible for the body to function without it. Abstinence then causes 'withdrawal symptoms', which is the body's reaction to the absence of the drug.

But 'addiction' is a relatively recent concept. A couple of centuries ago, the 'alcoholic' would have received no sympathy. Drunks were not seen as fundamentally different from minor criminals - they were, like everyone else, responsible for their own actions and only had themselves to blame for the consequences. It was only in the nineteenth century, with the advancement of the medical profession and the emergence of the Temperance movement that the notion of alcoholism as an illness began to take shape.

This was a rather humanitarian step, since alcoholics were not now seen as responsible for their condition. Some individuals, because of their constitution, were seen as particularly vulnerable to the addictive qualities of alcohol - they needed to take a drink only once or twice and they were 'hooked'. Alcoholism as an illness which required therapy thus came to replace the older moralistic view of the blameworthy drunk. We shall return to the example of alcoholism in the next section, but use it here as an illustration of the rise of the concept of addiction. We can see that this concept always entails two assumptions: first, addiction is a physical illness requiring a cure, and second, since the addict is ill they cannot reasonably be held totally responsible for their condition. You don't blame people for becoming ill, though you do expect them to do whatever is necessary to get better.

In recent years the concept of addiction has come to embrace an ever-increasing number of problems. As well as 'hard' and 'soft' drugs and alcohol, the nicotine in cigarettes, the caffeine in coffee and tea, and who knows how many food additives, have come to be seen as potentially addictive. And when we hear claims that addiction to coffee, or some other apparently harmless substance, does indeed exist, our reaction is likely to be twofold. We are horrified – after all, addiction is the nightmare, the *bête noire* of our time – but there is also a sense of relief. My claim that I cannot function adequately if 1 do not start the day with a pint of strong tea (and my subsequent irritability if this is for some reason prevented) becomes explicable. I am no longer to blame for my irritability, it is the result of my body's addiction. The relief is greater the more damaging or socially undesirable the addiction. Smoking is both of these, and although there is often great pressure upon people to give it up, the moral condemnation is ameliorated by the implicit assumption that smokers 'can't help themselves' – they are addicted to nicotine. This assumption is manifested in the current advertising of nicotine products which are supposed to help the 'addict' to withdraw from the drug gradually while taking it in a form which is not as damaging to their health (and that of others) as cigarettes.

In the rest of this chapter we shall argue that addiction does not represent a final and definitive explanation; rather, it can be seen as one way of construing certain problems, like smoking, but one which often creates more problems than it solves. We shall look at why it appears a more attractive alternative to the will-power/moral fibre alternative, but will also offer a psychological PCP construction of addiction which, we argue, has more utility than either the 'moral fibre' or biomedical alternatives.

Explanations in terms of 'addiction' are examples of reductionism; the phenomenon to be explained is 'reduced' to its constituent parts – we take it to pieces to see how all the different sub-parts work, then we work out how the whole thing works from our understanding of the behaviour of the smallest or lowest-order parts. These kinds of explanations have the appeal of all discoveries, as when we take apart our favourite clockwork toy, or kaleidoscope for the first time and exclaim 'So *that's* how it works!'. Such explanations have been very useful in the physical sciences and engineering, but we argue that they are not always appropriate for understanding how *people* work. The reader will already be familiar with our criticism of mechanistic explanations of human conduct and will recognise reductionism as belonging to the general realm of the mechanistic metaphor. But from the standpoint of constructive alternativism, we can see that although we can look at people as though they were biological machines, this is not the only perspective open to us; it is one view among many. We may also be construed as members of society, individuals with our own thoughts and feelings, created in God's image, or as a virus destroying the organism earth. It may, in many circumstances, be valuable to entertain the biomedical view – it would probably be dangerous to construe a case of appendicitis in any other way – but, it must not become what Kelly terms a 'pre-emptive construction'. This means that we must not become so attached to our biomedical construction of people that we say that, to all intents and purposes, we are nothing but biological machines. When this happens, virtually any human behaviour or experience becomes subjected to the same kind of analysis and the same kinds of answers are offered. Everything a person does, feels or thinks then becomes nothing more than a biological event acted out at the level of individual body cells or chemicals. It is essential that we remind ourselves that there are various levels of explanation for any event, any phenomenon, and the question is at what level is this phenomenon best understood? If we are dealing with a problem, we must ask what level of explanation gives us the best prescription for doing something about it.

When we are dealing with human conduct, there are various levels of reductionist explanation on offer. Behaviourism, the most influential school of psychological thought in the twentieth century, focused on simple units of animal behaviour in laboratory conditions and sought to construct a picture of complex human behaviour from these building blocks. However, such formulations have always been criticised, and increasingly former behaviourists have moved towards explanations in terms of constructivism and meaning (Mahoney, 1974; 1991) Explanations at the more molecular physiological level attempt to match a particular human action with, say, a particular brain state or hormonal change.

Of course, we could carry on relentlessly in our reductionistic search and try to explain physiological changes in terms of the atoms and molecules that make up organic carbon chains. Ultimately we might want to deal only in the speculative realms of subatomic physics, the mysterious forces that bind the universe together: after all, everything is made up of smaller parts. Our point is that once you start reducing, there is no natural or logical level at which to stop; you simply have to choose the 'most appropriate level of explanation, the particular construction that is most suitable.

Talk of addiction suggests that our actions can best be explained in physiological or biomedical terms; we eat, drink or smoke, and some process in our neurones and synapses explains why we want more. It also suggests that this wanting is unreasonable or self-damaging, at least in the eyes of others. One, rarely hears of addiction to vitamins, wholefoods, vegetables or low-fat spreads. We want something despite the fact that we know it is harmful. It is the failure of reason that calls for an explanation at a physiological level. Of course. it must be true that *something* is going on at a physiological level all the time: neurological pathways probably undergo changes every time a thought goes through our heads, we hear a sound or eat a peanut. If we like eating, doing or looking at something, no doubt this also is accompanied by chemical flux within us. But this does not mean that our preferences, our tastes, our likes and dislikes are best explained through a process of reductionism. For such an explanation to be taken seriously we would need at least to be able to correlate a specific psychological process with a specific physiologcal one. The argument for reductionist explanations has to be a deterministic one, that is, that any one psychological state is caused by a corresponding physiological one. The argument is null and void if the same physiological state can produce a variety of psychological states, but all too often this turns out to be the case. For example, in the field of emotions, research indicates that physiological arousal may manifest itself in any one of a number of emotional states, depending on the social circumstances at the time (e.g. Schacter and Singer, 1962). Drinking is also a good example. It is generally accepted that the effects of alcohol on one's emotional state vary enormously with the circumstances, and may run the gamut from deep depression to elation. So although autonomic nervous activity and the release of adrenaline may be a necessary precondition for the explanation of, say, the experience of anxiety, it is not sufficient. The same physiological state may give rise to excitement that is interpreted sometimes as euphoria, sometimes as anger and sometimes as panic. The key word here is 'interpret'. The person makes some sort of non-conscious judgement, based on the situation and on their own history, of what the arousal means. If someone knocks off a policeman's helmet after drinking eight pints of beer, drunkenness cannot be said to have caused this action – consumption of eight pints of beer does not *always* lead to this. Alcohol does not act directly upon those parts of the cerebral cortex responsible for the complicated motor and visual co-ordination needed to carry out the action. At best we can say that it suppresses inhibition. But then the wish that has hitherto been inhibited must be explained psychologically. No one suggests that beliefs, wishes or ideas can be simply translated into identifiable neurological activity. These phenomena are the properties of a different, psychological level of explanation, and it is organisation, complex interactions, that are lost when we reduce something to its constituent parts. We could not discover what was so haunting in a piece of music by examining each note out of context of the whole. No one can say why I am intensely irritated by the voice of a radio presenter by analysing the sound waves she emits. Similarly, no one can adequately explain why I compulsively eat chocolate every evening while watching television, or why my friend continues to smoke 20 cigarettes a day when he knows it is ruining his health and his lovely singing voice, by recourse to speculation about neurophysiology. So although it may be very tempting to take human behaviours to bits to see 'how they work', we argue that it is often not productive to try to explain events at a level other than that at which the event occurs, or is experienced: that which is experienced psychologically is often best explained and understood psychologically.

As we have seen, constructive alternativism allows us to shop around without obligation to buy, to look for new forms of explanation without discarding the old. In proposing a psychological construal of addiction, we do not deny physiological, or any other, constructions. Let us see what such a psychological formulation has to offer.

We begin by discarding the biomedical term 'addiction' and substituting it with 'dependence'. This linguistic strategy allows us to invite you to consider 'addictions' as special cases of a larger, more familiar and more everyday picture. All of us are dependent, in varying degrees, upon the people and things in our lives. This does not mean that we would expire without them, but that their loss would cause pain and disruption in our lives, and we should have to find ways of coming to terms with their loss in some way. But there is another side to this 'normal' dependency. The way we talk about dependencies is not morally neutral. It always entails an implicit, if not explicit, value judgement about what we regard, in our culture, as normal and reasonable. So it follows that when we say that someone is dependent we are not simply making a neutral description of them but judging them with a degree of (usually) disapproval. We may refer to a woman as 'dependent' in this derogatory fashion if she relies upon her husband for her keep, her social contacts and her self-esteem. But we should not take this view (in *our* society) of one who did not grow her own food, build her own house and mend her own car. So the first point is that we see some dependencies only because they show up against the background of our own cultural expectations. We are all dependent on others for some things, and indeed someone who could do without others altogether would be regarded as something of an antisocial freak. Some dependencies are assigned a positive value in our culture and are subtly encouraged. A man is jovially referred to as a 'workaholic', but rather than being characterised as weak willed (like the smoker who can't give it up) he is seen as having 'drive' and is awed and respected by his fellows – although, incidentally, the same tributes may not be paid so easily to a woman exhibiting the same behaviour.

This reflects the unspoken rules operating in society at large, and points to the fine line women must tread between being 'appropriately feminine' and, for example, 'over-dependent'. So there is no objective definition of dependence; in many respects 'it exists only in the eye of the beholder and represents a social judgement, not a fact. Looked at in this way, dependency is not a discrete physiological state that can be clearly and reliably distinguished from 'normal' or non-dependent states, but is a feature of much of our lives, varying in degree and subject to social value judgements.

As we have noted, we are most likely to call an activity 'addictive' when it is judged harmful or socially unacceptable, and we apply the term 'addict' to ourselves or others when the activity appears to be irrational, to make no sense. After all, who in their right mind would logically decide to carry on smoking/taking drugs/drinking excessively, etc.? The realms of physiology beckon seductively in our search for explanation. We have already met the issue of the 'logic of un-reason', and the same point is relevant here. When we begin to construe such problems psychologically, particularly when we adopt a PCP framework, we begin to see that there is always a 'psycho-logic' to people's behaviour. Behaviour may appear unreasonable and irrational from an observer's standpoint, but from within the system of construing used by the person doing the behaving his or her behaviour is meaningful and understandable. This is of vital importance once we get on to the possibilities for change – giving up cigarettes, drink, drugs, chocolate, coffee or anything else upon which we depend and wish we didn't. Any psychological construal of such problems must render the action meaningful to the actor for it to be useful. Once the action has been brought within the ambit of some psycho-logic, no matter how idiosyncratic, there is the possibility of exploring its psychological landscape and arriving at some fruitful intervention (we take up this point again in the next chapter).

So far we have invited you to consider an alternative construction of addiction, one that is better described by the term 'dependency', and which is a psychological rather than physiological construal. And as we are proposing a PCP view of dependency, we argue that it is the internal logic of a person's construing the meaning attached to their dependencies which holds the key to personal change. But there is another way in which PCP can lead us to a fruitful understanding of dependency. Within a Kellian framework, we do not see 'dependency' as a kind of personality trait, something that people have to a greater or lesser degree. Rather it has to do with the way in which the person construes the people and objects of their social world. From the time we are born, we are actively engaged in this process of construal, questioning, theory making, even though as babies and young children we do not have the language with which to represent these constructions to ourselves or others. Even though infants cannot ponder the idea of dependency, they are actively engaged in the process of sorting their world into 'dependable versus non-dependable' people and objects. The dependency constructs at first may be very simple, and consist of only one or two vital questions, such as 'who can I depend on to feed me when I'm hungry?', and in the case of infants (at least in our society) it is likely that there is a narrow range of answers to this question. The infant has, so to speak, all its eggs in one basket. It is only as it gets older that the infant's dependency constructs begin to admit more and more people, and the older child clearly spreads its dependencies among several people and things in a way that infants often do not.

In Kelly's terms, the dependency construct has become more 'permeable'. (A permeable construct is one that admits new elements (people or things) into its context.) One dependency construct might be 'Who or what can I depend on for moral support? while another might be 'Who or what will help me when I'm ill?'. Permeability means that new objects, people or activities can be incorporated into the dependency constructs, and hence relied upon. So the infant's dependency construing is impermeable when it relies upon a very limited range of resources, normally parents or other care-takers. Note that construing in the realm of dependency will certainly predate language and might remain largely non-verbal, so that we find it difficult to articulate or say on what we depend and why. Like so much vital, superordinate construing it remains as 'ground' rather than as 'figure' in our perception, rather as the fish, utterly dependent on water, may never come to realise it until landed in the fisherman's net.

Kelly suggests that the wise person distributes their dependencies as they develop – the eggs are placed in more than one basket. This increased permeability is highly functional of course, but sometimes may not occur, perhaps due to lack of opportunity or other circumstances, and then the person may find out how much and in what ways he depended on his wife, his job or early morning cup of tea only when it is lost to him. The 'withdrawal symptoms' of agitation and depression are likely to follow *any* major loss, whether of a drug or person or activity that we value and in some way depend upon in crucial areas of our lives. The fact that these 'symptoms' might well be physical, such as pains, crying, shivering, weight loss and so on, should not mislead us into seeking a physical cause. It is interesting to note here that gambling 'addicts', when trying to give up their dependency, suffer many of the same 'withdrawal symptoms' as the drug addict (see Heather and Robertson, 1986). From a Kellian perspective, this does not surprise us, since we have already cast doubt upon the utility of the 'physical versus mental' way of construing human experience. When people are in the process of coming to terms with major changes in their lives, fundamental and rapid reconstrual of themselves and their place in their world is required. It is hardly surprising if the emotional turmoil this creates involves mental/physical experiences of a sometimes dramatic nature. What we said earlier about 'constructs in transition' is exemplified here.

From a psychological point of view, we can foresee that people will be most vulnerable to dangerous 'addictions' when they are in some way lost, grieving or stressed. Nobody is independent. We all need support, help and alliances at some time or other. But when dependencies are seen as addictions, undue attention is focused on the substance, its addictive properties, and its physiological effects upon the person. This is seen as the link to break. But what about its function and meaning in the person's life, the relationships it is centred on, the social network it supports and holds together? If my 'TV chocolate-eating' is invested with notions of comfort security and well-being, it is not 'surprising that giving it up poses some difficulty, particularly if I have developed few alternative resources. For the man to whom heavy drinking is inextricably linked with virility, being 'one of the lads' and all that it entails, we should expect some problems when he attempts to become a teetotaller. The cigarette smoker who tries to give up is not simply faced with the prospect of doing without nicotine. When cigarette smoking has become part and parcel of the performance of a myriad of regular and important events in a person's life, from having a cup of coffee to eating a meal to making love, it is folly to suppose that a nicotine substitute will solve the problem. So when a person loses something she depends on, in whatever sense, whether it be cigarettes, a comfort blanket or an obnoxious and unreliable husband, we have to ask what losses this points to in the fine grain of the person's life, and what might be substituted for it. We can't just exhort people to 'stand on their own two feet'. A man who relies totally on his wife is widowed and he becomes anxious and depressed. He then becomes addicted to tranquillisers; certainly this addiction needs to be broken, but what will he put in its place? Only a psychological construal of the problem raises such issues, and a PCP approach directs our attention to the vital area of the meanings attached to dependencies for people.

In the next section of the book, we look at how PCP can cast light upon the process of attempting to change. We begin the section with a chapter which uses a case study in alcohol dependency as an illustration of the importance of meaning in understanding and treating the problem.

Chapter 15
Am I Traumatised?

These days, it is very common to hear people talk about being 'stressed out' by events and 'traumatised' by something that has happened to them. People sometimes ask whether contemporary life is more stressful than life was in some bygone era. Now, it seems to us very unlikely that this could be the case. Just imagine living in Victorian times, when infant mortality was high, children were routinely physically abused and women died regularly in childbirth. There were no anaesthetics to dull the pain of medical procedures (even if such procedures were available), poverty was extreme, pollution was everywhere and life expectancy was short. No health services or social security services were provided and those who couldn't keep themselves spent their last days in segregated workhouses in which conditions were worse than in modern prisons. And, of course, these early industrial conditions were an improvement on those in pre-modern times! No, it can't be the case that life is in any simple way more stressful today, and that more of us are traumatised by our childhood than was the case in even the recent past. Yet we do hear much more about stress and trauma today. Why is this?

One necessary condition is that there is now a readily available vocabulary for people to draw on in everyday life. We pick up a newspaper, turn on a TV or listen to a radio and we hear about harassment, trauma and stress. We hear that there has been a tragedy at a school, but that 'trained counsellors' are on hand to help anyone distressed by events. We watch a TV programme and are warned that anybody upset by it can contact a helpline where counsellors can advise the traumatised. The general public is now well acquainted with psychiatric terminology. Most people today have heard about anorexia, bulimia and obsessional-compulsive disorder as well as post-traumatic stress disorder (PTSD). So we now have a psychiatric framework ready at hand within which to interpret how we feel. Instead of feeling 'anxious' we are 'stressed out'. Whereas once we might have described ourselves as 'upset', we now talk about trauma. We find that what we thought were just upsetting memories are now called 'flashbacks' and that these are symptoms of post-traumatic stress disorder. We can see, then, that our experience is a construction as well as a discovery. We find how we feel about things by giving these feelings a shape, and this shaping comes from a vocabulary that is ready to hand. One of the basic functions of counselling and therapy is to help us by getting us to articulate our feelings and thus be able to work with them. And the terminology of counsellors and therapists has now become more widely available and drawn upon.

Of course, arguing that our experience is a discovery is not to say that it is in any way imaginary or made up. It simply means that it could have been put together differently, had it been interpreted within a different framework. So it is important to note that how we see things today is very different from how our forebears saw them. What we now designate as traumatic and stressful they dismissed and tried to ignore. In a recent TV documentary, a World War II veteran was interviewed about the stress of being a pilot in the Battle of Britain. 'We just got on with it – there was nothing else you could do' he said. Stoicism was admired; indeed necessary if you didn't want to be thought a coward by your comrades. 'Lack of moral fibre' was the explanation for those who broke down under the stress of battle. In World War I, things were even worse; soldiers who broke down in battle could be shot for cowardice in the face of the enemy. Contemporary psychiatrists would certainly diagnose most of these battle casualties as suffering from post-traumatic stress disorder. So we can see that the same event (battle stress) can be construed in either moral or medical terms. A deviation from moral norms results in punishment, whereas a deviation from medical norms leads to diagnosis and treatment. The American psychiatrists' Diagnostic and Statistical Manual for Mental Disorders (DSM) recognised PTSD as a psychiatric illness for the first time only in 1980. The DSM says that it has been called shell-shock or battle fatigue syndrome. The symptoms of PTSD are:

- *Intrusion*. The sufferer is said to constantly re-experience the trauma. They go over and over traumatic events in their minds in a way that is said to be different from just remembering. It is claimed that it is as though the trauma were actually happening again. The term 'flashbacks' is used to describe this aspect of experience, bringing to mind the way in which films use this technique when a character is reliving or remembering the past vividly.
- *Avoidance.* Sufferers avoid situations that might trigger the intense emotions associated with flashbacks. Their preoccupation with the

trauma can also lead to an avoidance of intimacy and contact. This 'numbing' of feeling and distance from others can result in depression.

- *Hyperarousal*. Emotional numbness might alternate with heightened emotional expression. Increased anxiety, irritability and emotional explosiveness are said to be characteristic of PTSD sufferers, leading to insomnia, depression and drug or alcohol abuse.

There is surely no doubt that it is more humane to treat people within a psychiatric or medial framework than in a moral one, where people are blamed for their responses to extreme situations. Nonetheless, the implications of this approach raise many problems from a constructivist point of view. For PTSD to be diagnosed, the patient has to have experienced or witnessed a threat to life or safety. Having the disorder is dependent on an objective description of a situation that you have been involved in. Of course, psychiatrists realise that not everybody who is exposed to a life-threatening event will suffer PTSD. But this is a necessary condition for the diagnosis. What PCP stresses is that the difference between those who do and those who don't suffer from PTSD must be due to differences in the construction processes in different people. It follows that what a person finds traumatic cannot be simply described objectively. I might survive a serious car injury that is life threatening, but develop no symptoms at all; but then I may be traumatised when I am rejected by an old friend, or when my dog dies. From a constructivist point of view, the reason for this lies in the disturbance caused in my construct system by events, and not by the events themselves.

It is this aspect of disrupted construction that has been taken up by Sewell and his colleagues (Sewell et al., 1996; Sewell, 1997, 2003). Working mainly with veterans of the Vietnam War, Sewell emphasises that what happens in PTSD is that the sufferer's world of assumptions and anticipations is badly shaken by the events with which they have been confronted. Each of us develops a narrative (or as Sewell terms it, a 'metaconstruction') that binds the past, present and future together for us. We can carry on without thinking too much in normal everyday life precisely because we have such a narrative. And central to this is a narrative or theory about ourselves. I tell myself I'm this sort of person and not that sort, based on how I story my past and how I expect to act in the future. It is these stories or narratives that are destroyed by a traumatic event. It is then that nothing makes sense and the person loses their grip on things as their anticipations break down. Sewell (1997, p. 232) gives us an example of a client who found himself acting in ways that he could not later understand.

After working Joe through a recounting of his traumatic experiences, our therapy group listened intently as he read a letter he had written to a village in Vietnam – a letter that could not be sent because Joe had killed everyone there. In the letter, he apologised and tried to explain his state of mind. He asked permission to go on living. Then Joe cried.

People like Joe who have experienced or committed atrocities frequently find that their actions just do not seem to belong to them. They act in the heat of the moment and then cannot own their actions. In the face of what Sewell (1997) calls 'constructive bankruptcy', the person then has three possible strategies. First, they may dissociate – forget or deny the traumatic incident, try to ignore it and carry on as before. As we saw above, this was the only way many men saw as a possible way of coping in World War II. Second, they may scrap their past system of construction and see everything in terms of the trauma; everything becomes dangerous. After a rape, a woman may come to see every man as a threat and all interactions with them impossible. Third, they may just constrict their thinking and activities, become depressed, and refuse to face the world at all.

So constructivists emphasise the sufferer's construction of the event rather than the event itself. It is the meaning of the event that matters, and PCP always underlines the fact that the same event will surely mean different things to different people. Of course, faced with dreadful circumstances, most people will find their systems of meaning-making severely challenged. But when we talk of trauma 'impacting' on us, we are left in the position of passive sufferers who have no control at all over their circumstances. It is always a mistake to assume that something in the past causes us to be the way we are now. It is just as true to say that we make our histories as much as it is to assert that they make us. We make our histories through developing narratives that we tell others and ourselves (See Chapter 9). Neimeyer (2002) argues that traumatic memories are constructed under conditions of high arousal that prevent them being assimilated into other narrative structures. Their integration (which results in the person making some sense of the trauma) depends on their being reprocessed and hence brought under control. Like Sewell (1997) he suggests that therapy involves a process of re-narration, in which the therapist works with the client to encourage a new telling of the traumatic story. The stance of constructive alternativism makes us recognise that it is always possible – if not always easy – to find different perspectives on the things that have happened to us. Of course, this doesn't mean that you can wish circumstances away and interpret things in any way you want. Marx is often quoted as saying that people make history, but not in circumstances of their own choosing. Some have far more adverse circumstances to cope with than others.

Clearly, one potentially traumatic event for anyone is the death of a loved one, or the impending death of yourself. Grief is expressed very differently in different societies. Until very recently it was thought that the English expressed grief in a much more stoical way than did those in the eastern Mediterranean (Harré and Gillett, 1994). Then the death of Diana Princess of Wales in 1997 showed that the English way of grieving appeared to be changing rapidly. No longer did people grieve quietly and privately, even for someone they knew only through the media. We might expect that the increased show of emotion would be even more extreme when the loss is less remote. Now, there are likely to be many things contributing to this change in practice. Perhaps one is that what was once 'common sense' about grief has changed. The stoical attitude that was implicitly recommended in the face of adversity extended to facing trauma and grief. But since the late 1970s a different understanding of grief has gradually taken hold. Originating in the psychoanalytic work of John Bowlby, it was elaborated by Parkes and Kübler-Ross. This theory posited a number of stages of the grief process. So when a person is faced with their own death, it was proposed that they progressed through a particular sequence:

- Denial: The person just refuses to believe that this is happening to them.
- Anger: A feeling of 'why me?' predominates in this stage.
- Bargaining: Here, the person clings to the hope that they can change in some way and survive.
- Depression: It finally dawns on the person that they really are going to die.
- Acceptance: It is hoped that the person finally reaches this stage in the grieving process.

A similar set of stages ranging from denial to acceptance, was thought to be associated with the grieving for a loved one.

R.A. Neimeyer (2002) has extensively researched grief from a constructivist standpoint. He points out that the stage theory above has many limitations and problematic implications. To begin with, it assumes that everyone ought to go through the same stages in the same order. If somebody doesn't go through an angry stage, we might think they ought to, and if they don't, they must be encouraged to. This is based on the idea that death means the same thing to everybody, and of course, it doesn't. Attachments to other people, and to one's own life, are subject to a whole range of personal constructions. If you think your death will lead you to paradise because you are about to die in the service of your faith, it will mean something entirely different from someone for whom death is the ultimate finality. There is therefore nothing necessarily pathological about grief that doesn't follow the exact stages prescribed above. And neither should there be an emphasis on the efficient return to 'normal' functioning. As Neimeyer points out, we never say goodbye to someone we lose; we remember them, carry on internal conversations with them and remain influenced by them long after their death. So our life is transformed by those to whom we are attached, and continues to be transformed after a loss. It is not that we merely accept the loss and move on, 'getting back to normal'. Constructivist therapy emphasises not only the loss-oriented approach that is characteristic of the psychoanalytic model, but also a restoration-oriented approach to complement it. This involves encouraging the client to undertake new activities, explore new roles and a general distraction from grief. Grievers then, not passive in the face of trauma that impact on them. Instead, they actively make sense of life and loss. Of course, complicated attachments can lead to complicated grieving, and therapists and counsellors have a useful role to play when this is the case. As in the case of trauma generally, our life narratives can become dislocated and disorganised, resulting in the problematic strategies that Sewell (1997) noted. Neimeyer notes that a sudden or violent death that rocks the person's assumptive world is likely to prove traumatic and hence involve complicated grief for anyone. But certain individuals are predisposed to complicated grief on the basis of their particular vulnerabilities and attachment styles.

So we can see that the emphasis on trauma today is, from a constructivist point of view, both a good and a bad thing. It is good in that it recognises how what happens to people hurts them; it isn't that they are just weak or oversensitive when they break down in the face of events. But it is bad (or at least misleading) because it over-simplifies what it means when something 'happens' to us. This 'happening' is mediated by a system of meaning-making that strives to construct and make sense of things. It is when it cannot do this that we see the phenomenon of trauma.

Part IV
Reconstruing Change

The central themes running through the chapters in this part are agency, choice and reconstrual. Kelly emphasised that people are always 'doing' something – even doing nothing is doing something! The dynamic, active nature he gives humankind goes hand in hand with the idea of human beings as agents of their own behaviour, having ultimate control over their actions through the decisions, the choices, they make. This is not to deny that people are often hamstrung by the restrictions of their own physical circumstances, but within those limitations, people make choices from among courses of action they perceive to be open to them. This last point is important, since one person's construal of a situation will not necessarily suggest the same array of choices that would be suggested by another's construal. And when the choices to be made concern personal change, we shall see that what a person decides to do has as much to do with what they fear they will lose as with what they hope they will gain.

Another important aspect of PCP which we examine in this section, as in the previous one, is that of the role of meaning in the choices we make, and indeed in our psychology generally. For example, in Chapter 16, 'Do I *Really* Want to Give Up Drinking?', we learn that we have to understand the meaning that drinking holds for a person, how it is tied into people's concepts of themselves and what it signifies in their social life, before we can map out the consequences for them in giving it up. So we are presenting a primarily psychological, PCP model of 'addictive' behaviour such as drinking, which contrasts with the prevalent biomedical approach and with other psychological models such as conditioning theories.

The issue of meaning is again raised in Chapter 18. In a series of examples, we explore how we may learn more about why people fail to benefit from experience, by examining the meaning their experiences hold for them, than by adopting simple common-sense personality or learning theory models.

As stated above, Kelly firmly believed that when a person does undergo real personal change, for example giving up smoking or becoming more assertive, it is that person him- or herself who is at the controlling centre of such change. Therapists, psychiatrists, psychologists and others may function as catalysts or guides, but it is not they who are bringing about the change. The issue of agency in therapy is illustrated in Chapter 17, and this chapter also shows the importance of 'as if' in therapy – the licence, inherent in most therapeutic relationships, given to the client to explore freely other ways of being, other parts of themselves, without fear of ridicule or censure.

Chapter 16
Do I *Really* Want to Give Up Drinking?

To deny that addiction' is the only way of explaining dependency problems is not to deny that they are indeed serious problems: giving up or cutting down smoking or excessive drinking is clearly in the interests of good health. But people frequently feel themselves to be helplessly in the grip of dependence. It feels as though they have no choice but to submit to the demands of their habit, in the absence of enough resolve to break with it. This is why we proposed, in Chapter 14, that they often receive the 'addiction' explanation with ambivalence. On the one hand 'addiction' is a serious matter and the 'cures' do not always work, so the prospects for the future may be grim. But, on the other hand, people cannot be wholly blamed for their addictions. While there may be a degree of moral responsibility attached to the decision to *start* smoking/drinking/gambling, etc., once the addiction is established people cannot be blamed for being unable to help themselves. The benefit of biomedical accounts is that everyone will agree that you are in the grip of something much bigger than you, and that you have the right to expect help and advice, as well as the duty to follow doctor's orders.

Now, if you assume the identity of 'addict', you might think you can bypass the problem of responsibility. At first sight it appears that you become a patient instead of someone who ought to pull themselves up by their own bootstraps. When people go to the doctor, they want to feel better, and ideally would like some medicine which would abolish their symptoms. In the case of addiction, they would like their wanting, their craving, to go away. A popular request is for hypnotherapy. The belief often underlying this request is that the hypnotist, through their special skills, addresses some inner man, some homunculus at the control centre, who can be persuaded to throw the appropriate switches and set a new course. There is a strong wish to feel better without having to take part in any way in the treatment – a dialogue between the hypnotist and the homunculus will sort it out. The patient wants simply to wake up with their craving miraculously removed. But agency cannot be buried so easily, unfortunately. There is no easy way out. Certainly there may be medicine, behavioural techniques or various remedies from the chests of alternative medicine of which addicts can avail themselves; but in the end, talk of 'being committed' to the treatment and of 'taking responsibility for the outcome' inevitably emerges. As we have noted earlier, there is broad agreement that real and lasting change is possible only when a person feels that they are an agent, an effective force directing their own psychological progress.

To talk of agency and taking responsibility for one's own personal change may sound like we are advocating that the 'addict' should be held responsible for their plight, and have only themselves to blame. This is certainly the only alternative to the biomedical explanation that is usually on offer to people. The biomedical view is popular partly because it reflects the culturally prevailing preference for mechanistic and reductionist explanations, and partly because it is more compassionate than the other perceived alternative. This is the 'will-power' option; most people will have tried and failed with this one before they accept or recognise that they are addicts, and this reconstrual of their problem seems to them more like a discovery of the 'real' state of affairs than a shift of perspective. It feels like they have discovered a physiological, 'fact'. But the obvious problem with will-power is where you get it from and why it so often deserts you in your hour of need! You hear extraordinary stories of other people's self-denial, but cannot imagine how they could apply to you. You hear of people who, perhaps after some dire health warning from, their doctor, have resolved to give up cigarettes or drink, and have never touched one since. But in your own case, will-power is present only when you don't need it. Immediately after a drinking session you can resolve to stop or cut down. The next day, the resolve melts and the will-power vanishes. 'Just one more'... 'I'll start tomorrow'... 'I must be terribly weak-willed – or perhaps I'm an addict?'. Most of us, in this sense, are too 'weak-willed' even to keep our most modest of New Year's resolutions. The will-power explanation puts everything down to our individual responsibility, whereas with 'addiction' we are passive victims requiring treatment.

In the rest of this chapter we shall put forward a way of construing dependency which does not rely on either physiological reductionism or will-power. We shall see why it is an illusion to suggest that resolve and grim determination are the key to personal change (though changing is always a difficult task) and why we have to understand fully the psychological and social implications of change for a person before change becomes a possibility.

When a person wants a drink or a cigarette, but at the same time wants to give it up, they are in conflict. They want incompatible things. We live in a society where every appetite is stimulated and titillated, and we should like to give in to the Siren's call. But we also want to be free of heart disease, lung cancer and liver failure. On the face of it, it seems as though the decision is a simple one. Do we want the short-term delights or our health? It appears that we are refusing to acknowledge the consequences of our behaviour and that someone could justifiably say to us 'Look, what do you *really* want?', as if it were a matter of balancing scales and observing where the weight falls. But no one is in a position to furnish a simple answer to such a question. The way it is asked makes it seem as though we can discover the answer through introspection: we look inside ourselves, read some internal meter and report on our findings. As we noted in earlier chapters, people are often unable to articulate what they want. Their desires, hopes, fears and needs are an expression of their construing, construing which may be so central to the way they perceive themselves and their social world that they cannot 'see' it; it is 'ground' rather than 'figure' for them. And many of the constructs we use in our daily lives can throw us into a state of internal conflict because they appear inconsistent. A person who construes themselves along the dimensions of 'responsible–irresponsible' and 'punctual–always late' will experience some degree of conflict when breaking the speed limit in order to attend an important meeting. This is something we are all used to, and the conflict experienced by someone who cannot reconcile their views of themselves as 'always ready to join the lads for a drink' and 'a good husband' is only different in its scale. Inconsistencies occur all the time, and are noticed only when circumstances lead to a crisis or collision, when some decision must be taken. The person must decide which needs are superordinate, and this can be done only by unravelling the myriad implications for their life attached to their construing. If 'responsible–irresponsible' also implies 'boringly predictable–innovative' it will figure very differently in prescriptions for change than if it implies 'good friend–doesn't care'.

The essential feature of change looked at in this way is that it *does* involve a decision, a choice. We cannot appeal to any book of rules or an internal oracle to help us; there is no internal fount of wisdom, and self-knowledge is not meter reading. Choice is never easy and to say a course of action is chosen does not imply that we are happy with our choice. We are often faced with dilemmas and have to choose between two unpleasant options. Any decision might entail unseen costs as well as benefits, and there may well be a great deal to come to terms with.

So a person has to understand the meanings attached to their dependency before the process of decision-making and choice can begin. The first step must be for the person to establish their aims, to get them to decide what is at issue, to work out where they are prepared to go. It is not a question of what they *really* want, but of decision. The problem cannot be tackled by looking into the depths or into the past, but only by looking into the future. If we see dependence as an illness, as addiction, the aims are already pre-empted; no decision is required. People must get rid of their addiction, they surely *want* to give it up, but when dependence is appreciated as part of the fabric of your life, part of a larger picture rather than as a discrete disease entity, the implications for change can begin to be assessed. As you throw away your drink and say 'Right, that's it. I've finished with it', you could not be further from the truth: you have just begun. What will you do when you deserve a break after a hard day or when commiserating with the next-door neighbour? How will you structure your life now? What is there to look forward to? At the end of each day will you say 'One day down and the rest of my life to get through! What's the point?'? It seems to us entirely appropriate to view the loss of any dependency, such as alcohol, cigarettes, gambling, and even in many cases 'hard' drugs, as involving the same kinds of implications for a person as the loss from their life of important people, whether through death, divorce or other means. We can ask to what extent giving up their dependency is like the death of an old friend, the loss of a marriage partner or job. In the event of any of these losses, it is generally accepted that to say 'Oh well, (he/she/it) is gone now; I must simply try to forget about it' would constitute denial. One just does not expect to 'get over' such losses by trying to ignore them and carry on as if nothing had happened. Appropriate grief work and mourning would be seen as a necessary part of coming to terms with the loss, and that in time the person would evolve a new way of life, a new picture of themselves and their world which did not include the lost person. People do carry on after truly dreadful loss – of health, sight, loved ones, but it is never quick, easy or without pain or adjustment.

Both loss and dependence must be defined in subjective terms, in terms of individual construing. Two people whose mothers die do not suffer the same loss. The difference may be subtle or gross, but the maternal relationship will not be exactly the same, and therefore neither can be their losses. How well they cope will depend on what this relationship constituted for them, as well as what other relationships and supports are now available to them. In just the same way, two people giving up drinking are not giving up the same thing.

Many losses are thrust upon us: we have no choice but to endure them. But many are the result of our decisions, and in this respect resemble giving up drinking or smoking. Sometimes we end a relationship, petition for divorce, or leave the parental home. Such decisions invariably involve ambivalence: 'I can't live with her, but I can't live without her' is a not uncommon sentiment. So a realistic appraisal of our 'ability' to give up something must hinge upon successful anticipation. What is going to matter in the days, weeks, months and years ahead? Will you be prepared to pay the price? It is as well to be able to foresee difficulties in dealing with physical or psychological pain. Forewarned is to some extent forearmed. At least you are not in for nasty shocks that demoralise you and sap your strength to go on.

In Chapter 5 we described how Kelly saw the decision process as involving a three-stage cycle. In 'circumspection' we take a walk around the psychological landscape, and get a feel for all the issues that are at stake for us in this particular decision; this is followed by 'pre-emption', when we decide which of these issues are crucial to us and which peripheral; the third stage, 'control', denotes our action in the light of this pre-emption. So it is clear that for a good decision, one which we will be able to carry through in our lives, pre-emption must not be whimsical, but must be based upon a great deal of insight into the gains and losses implied for us in our decision. However, it is often the case that, although people can usually quite readily spell out the advantages (as they see them) of change, they often have more difficulty with forecasting its disadvantages, the costs of change. Yet it is vitally important that these too be articulated and entered into the person's psychological 'cost–benefit' analysis. Tschudi (1977) devised a good method for examining the network of implications involved in choice. An individual is encouraged to express their complaint and their desire for change in terms of bipolar constructs. Let us examine how this works with the example of a case study.

Joe was an alcoholic: at least that was how he described himself. He accepted the conventional wisdom that the only 'cure' for his 'illness' was total abstinence. Unhappily, though, he had suffered several relapses. Using Tschudi's scheme, Joe was able to elaborate his construing as follows:

Choice	Disadvantages	Advantages
Stay alcoholic	I'm a drunk – a no-good; My wife will leave me; I'll lose my job; I'll be broke; I'll be just a wimp.	
Give it up		Sober, I'd be a useful member of society; I'd save my marriage; I'd keep my job; I'd have money; It will prove I have will-power.

So far, so good. But, like most of us looking for radical change in our lives, Joe was at first unable to see the other side of the picture, what he would lose in such change, and other undesirable (from his point of view) consequences. A careful examination of his 'relapses' revealed the following important features:

Choice	Disadvantages	Advantages
Stay alcoholic		At least I can go to the pub; I can be the sort of person who 'lives for the day'.
Give it up	Won't have a social life; I'll be boring.	

Unless the disadvantages, the obstacles to change, are tackled, Joe is going to be constantly threatened by an alcoholic problem. To an onlooker with different values, Joe's construct system might make no sense at all. But the fact remains that this is his way of seeing things, and these are the implications as far as he's concerned. His drinking cannot be comprehended by examining his brain state or physiology; it has to be seen as a way of life. Giving up drinking means, to him, giving up his social life (as he construes it) and the most important aspects of his self-image. Not only will he have nowhere to go of an evening, but he'll become one of those dull, semi-detached types who are attached to their wife's apron strings.

There was no doubt that Joe ought to stop drinking. Apart from anything else, his health was deteriorating and his doctor had informed him that his liver would not take much more abuse (though interestingly this does not feature prominently in his lists of priorities).

The disadvantages of giving up alcohol are probably not insurmountable, although we should not underrate them. The worst thing that we can do is to dismiss them and say, 'Oh, come on, as if *that's* important when your life's at stake!'. Unless we can begin by seeing things through his eyes, Joe is a dead man.

Chapter 17
Can You Really Hypnotise People?

Hypnosis occupies a somewhat precarious position on the map of psychological theory and research. It has been the subject of a great deal of serious psychological study, particularly in the USA and yet its apparent nature finds it classified upon library shelves with 'the occult', 'magic' and 'ESP'. Its image, fuelled by the media and entertainment industries, does not allow it to take its place easily beside such worthy topics as 'learning' or 'motivation'. Thus, in the minds of many psychologists as well as other people, hypnosis is less likely to be thought of alongside other aspects of everyday behaviour and experience and tends to crop up more in conversations which begin 'Do you believe in...' and end in 'ghosts' and 'UFOS'.

The reason for this is simple. Hypnosis appears to be one of those phenomena which, if not the result of trickery or illusion, cannot be explained with recourse to known psychological or physical principles. It is mysterious, powerful and inexplicable. There is something very appealing in this kind of idea. Like other 'mysteries', from precognition to the Bermuda Triangle, there is the suspicion that there are powers of nature at work of which we are unaware, or only dimly aware; that there are untapped resources of power hidden deep within human beings which may be unleashed under special circumstances. It is almost akin to religious belief, since it subscribes to a view of human beings as driven by and subject to powerful forces which we as yet cannot, or cannot ever, know. The appeal of this lies in the opportunity it gives us to believe in the possibility for human beings to transcend ordinary mundane experience, to be part of something greater and more fundamental than mere existence. This is a philosophical and religious issue which we do not propose to debate here. We simply, offer it as an explanation for the resistance that has been encountered by those trying to bring hypnosis within the realm of ordinary explanation – it is as if people feel they are being told that Santa Claus does not exist. The result has been that researchers of hypnosis who have attempted to demystify it and bring it within the realm of ordinary experience and explanation have often met with hostility and redoubled efforts to prove the existence of some special state of consciousness or 'hypnotic trance'. It seems as though in questioning the almost mystical quality of hypnosis, by characterising it as merely a special case of 'compliance' or 'motivation', the reality of the phenomenon is also being denied.

In this chapter we intend to tread the tightrope between mysticism and scepticism. We wish to bring hypnosis firmly within the realm of psychological explanation but without playing down the reality and potency of the phenomenon. We shall offer an explanation of hypnosis which reveals some unhelpful assumptions in traditional psychological thinking, assumptions which lead to the posing of essentially unanswerable questions, such as the one in the title.

Let us then first describe the character of hypnosis and the hypnotic situation as it is traditionally seen. Hypnosis is seen as requiring the participation of two people, hypnotist and subject. The use of the term 'subject' tells us that the relationship is based on unequal degrees of power. Thus the hypnotist is seen as in a position of power and authority with respect to the subject. This powerfulness may furthermore be seen as a *property* of the hypnotist, i.e. part of his or her personality, rather than endowed as part of the role of hypnotist. So a hypnotist is often thought of as having some power or particular charismatic quality by virtue of which they are able to practise hypnosis. The logical follow-on from this is that, by the exertion of this special power, the hypnotist is able to induce in the subject a state of hypnotic trance. Once in this state, the subject is stripped of their self-control or will-power, and is entirely 'in the power' of the' hypnotist.

While many researchers of hypnosis would smile at this rather theatrical discription, it is underlain by an important psychological assumption. This is that hypnosis may be understood solely at the level of individual psychology: individuals enter a hypnotic state and are caused to do so by the operation of particular psychological characteristics of the hypnotist. Explanations of hypnosis are therefore also rooted at this level: 'What kinds of people can hypnotise others?' 'What psychological events define the hypnotic state?.' 'Are some personalities more hypnotisable than others?'

'Can you really hypnotise people?' is one of these questions. The answers it invites concern the issues of whether hypnosis is real or fake, of whether a hypnotist really has any special powers or is just manipulating the gullible. The question focuses on how we should characterise the individual psychological state of subject or hypnotist, or both. However, these long-standing issues have not been settled by the mass of experimental research which they have generated. Consistent physiological conditions chara-c-terising the 'hypnotic trance' have not been found, nor have researchers succeeded in identifying any personality characteristics which reliably discriminate between 'good' and 'poor' hypnotic subjects, or between those who are able to attain a 'deep' rather than 'light' trance state.

This very terminology is consistent with a prevalent, and, we argue, misleading assumption in psychology which has gained more or less universal acceptance. This is the idea that our psychological make-up is like a series of layers, some deeper and some more superficial than others. We see ourselves as having no route of access to the 'deep' layers of our personality. Only by the use of special devices and tools (the property of experts) such as hypnosis or psychotherapy can the doors be unlocked for us, revealing capacities, experiences and perhaps even memories that we normally cannot know. Hypnotherapy is usually characterised as the unlocking of psychological mechanisms by which people can gain control over aspects of their lives (for example stopping smoking or overcoming anxiety) while asleep.

To sum up so far then, we are accustomed to a notion of hypnosis which sees it as a highly unusual and out of the ordinary experience. It is brought about in individuals by the expert operation of other individuals who are in a relatively powerful position, and who are able to unlock psychological doors for the subject. The subject's responses are non-volitional, since power resides in the hypnotist. Within this framework, our answer to the question 'Can you really hypnotise people?' is firmly *no*.

However, we do not deny the reality of the hypnotic experience, and now put forward a PCP view of hypnosis which allows us to acknowledge the validity of hypnosis and hypnotherapy without lumbering ourselves with the problems entailed in the traditional model. As we noted earlier, evidence for a special 'trance' state does not exist, nor do we have any reason to believe that some 'types' of person are more hypnotisable than others (the reader will anyway by now be fully aware of our misgivings about traditional views of personality). Instead, more recent research in hypnosis invites us to consider an altogether different model of the phenomenon, one which brings it within the realms of our normal psychological and social functioning. The key to this lies in the nature of the normal imaginative-fantasy episodes which punctuate our lives. In novels, in films and plays, in poetry, music and a variety of other areas we temporarily enter into a realm of experience that is separate from our 'real' lives. We enter a world of events, thoughts and feelings which, although they are not 'really' happening, involve and engage us in a very real way. Most people would deny that the enjoyment and satisfaction they derive from such activities is simply due to their 'escape value', or role as time-fillers. No, when we are gripped with enthusiasm about the good novel we have just read, we are referring to something altogether different. Our 'good book' has invited us to sample another mode of experience, perhaps a different way of life in different circumstances. It has invited us to explore feelings and thoughts of which we may previously have been only dimly aware. Through this 'make-believe' world we find ourselves able to explore the extremities of our own psyche, to consider the possibilities of undreamed-of actions, and all this within the safe confines of our armchair!

So make-believe, the world of 'as if', affords us, in everyday life, opport-unities to go beyond the confines of our immediate circumstances, to explore corners of our souls we hide from the world, to elaborate and give full weight to aspects of ourselves we often cannot safely explore in our day-to-day lives. This lack of 'safety' exists perhaps in the form of social constraints on some kinds of behaviour, or it may take the form of the threat and insecurity we feel when we consider the possibility of being a different kind of person. Perhaps we see ourselves as 'submissive' and would like to be more 'assertive'. But the costs are dear, in real life, of gaily throwing off our familiar ways of being and stepping into ... who knows what? Who has not, in imagination, 'practised' some confrontational encounter, playing out in their mind's eye the possibilities of different scenarios? So the first point we are making is that the world of 'as if' is an important part of our normal lives, and affords us opportunities for safe exploration which are of benefit to us in tackling life's problems, from returning faulty merchandise to becoming a more confident person.

To return to the issue of hypnosis, the link here is that research from a variety of sources has demonstrated that 'good' subjects, people who seem able to make best use of hypnotic suggestions and easily experience the suggested effects, are doing so by the use of the same kinds of imaginative strategies. The good subject enters into the make-believe spirit of hypnotic suggestion uncritically, and under this 'safe umbrella' freely allows themselves to explore the possibilities for thought, feeling and experience that the hypnotist (like the author) suggests. So we are now at a point of seeing hypnosis not as something abnormal and unusual, but as the harnessing of a mode of thought or psychological functioning which is part of our normal, everyday lives.

The next step is to divest ourselves of the unhelpful 'depth' idea. Once we cease to view hypnotic experience as the unlocking of deep-seated parts of our personality and to see it as having more in common with our experience of reading a good novel, we can begin to take on an alternative view both of hypnosis and of our own psychology.

Rather than thinking of ourselves in terms of layers, some deep and some superficial, Mair (1977) suggests that we think of ourselves as a community.

The advantage of a metaphor like this is that it opens up possibilities that are closed to us if we hold on to the 'depth' idea. As a community, we are free to 'give voice' to little-heard 'minorities' in our make-up, to explore the dusty corners that are never given the chance to see the light of day. Thus hypnosis may be seen as an opportunity to try out different experiences, emotions and behaviour, different ways of being, from the safety of the therapist's couch. Kelly saw this world of 'as if', of exploration of alternative selves, as vital in the process of transition in personal change. We should not want to emigrate to another country without visiting it first to see what living there would be like! No special powers, techniques or states of mind are necessary for this, but we *do* need to feel safe; like a toddler exploring the cupboard under the sink, we need to feel that we can retreat to a place of safety should we find anything threatening.

This is especially true of the person who seeks personal change, and hypnosis provides a particularly useful 'safe umbrella' in this respect. This safety is provided in the form of what may be referred to as 'hypnotic licence'. Because of the way in which hypnosis is commonly conceptualised, i.e. that the subject is in the power of the hypnotist and cannot do other than what he or she suggests, this is just the excuse that people may need in order to venture into unknown and potentially threatening corners of their psyche – if anything untoward should happen, if they should break down, look a fool or lose control of themselves, at least there is the comforting knowledge that it is not they but the hypnotist who is 'doing' it! The power of this hypnotic licence should not be underestimated.

However, there is a price to be paid for this. A person who longs for change, who wants to stop smoking, stop overeating, become more confident, and who looks to therapy (including hypnotherapy) as the vehicle for this change, must in the end acknowledge their own central role in bringing it about. Kelly saw people not as passive organisms moulded and shaped by environmental forces, but as constantly actively engaged in the process of constructing their own self. Thus change is essentially in one's own hands, and one has to *choose* to change. This way of thinking has been taken on board more recently by various psychologists writing about therapy and personal change, and there is broad agreement that real and lasting change is achieved only when a person feels they are an agent, an effective force directing their own psychological progress. As we have argued elsewhere (Burr and Butt, 1989), hypnosis as a therapeutic tool stands to increase its usefulness by recognising this, by playing down the traditional 'non-volitional' view of hypnotic responding and instead presenting hypnosis to clients as a tool that will enable them to explore and elaborate parts of themselves they normally leave shut up in the attic. This idea would be very facilitative for many people who fear hypnosis because they are terrified of losing their will-power and self-control.

The role of the hypnotist needs to be examined here. If she or he has no special powers and does not put the subject/client into a special state, can the hypnotist be dispensed with altogether? We can answer this question by tackling the assumption, outlined earlier in this chapter, that hypnosis is something which happens at the level of the individual, that it happens within individuals and is caused by other individuals. But this notion virtually ignores the social context of hypnosis. Let us rather conceptualise hypnosis as something that happens *between* people, as a joint venture. The hypnotist-subject relationship can be seen to have strong similarities to the therapist-client relationship, and even to the author-reader relationship. Neither therapy nor the enjoyment of a story is possible without the mutual co-operation of two people. In the case of therapy, both therapist and client know implicitly the rules of the therapy game. They know what each is allowed and expected to do. We can say that in the therapy room these two individuals occupy the roles of therapist and client. This in no way means they are pretending to be therapist and client, but that they have undertaken a silent agreement on a form of interaction which is expected to enable the one to help the other by exploring, guiding and suggesting. The client needs the therapist in perhaps the same way as the reader needs the author - as a guide and mentor in a strange new world. We can think of the hypnotist-subject relationship in this way too. Both know the 'rules' of the game, they are aware of the behavioural and experiential possibilities inherent in their reciprocal roles. They are jointly engaged in a primarily interpersonal, social, but rule-bound venture in which the hypnotist/ therapist/author invites the subject/client/reader to accompany them on a safe adventure into the unknown.

Chapter 18
Why Don't They Ever Learn?

One of the most significant features of human beings which distinguishes us from other animals is our remarkable capacity for learning and adaptation. We are capable of learning the most complex skills. Even the relatively mundane activities of using a typewriter or following a knitting pattern are remarkable feats of co-ordination of hand, eye and thought. The nature of much of our learning is by trial and error and by observation. We learn both by observing the effects of our own behaviour (feedback) and by observing what other people do (modelling). Our learning capacity, our flexibility and adaptability have been held to be the most important factors in our rise to supremacy.

But if we are so good at learning from our mistakes, how do we account for those individuals who just never seem to learn? If we learn by adopting those behaviours which reward us (reinforcement) and by avoiding those that are noxious to us (negative reinforcement), why is it that some criminals repeatedly return to prison? Can't they *learn* to behave in a socially acceptable way? This is not only a problem in the adult world; before corporal punishment in schools was made illegal, how many teachers were heard to say 'Its always the same few who come back for a caning'? What is the matter with them, can't they *learn*?

In the same way, some people never seem to have learned the way to get on with others. Their social interactions are fraught with embarrassment because they don't seem to have caught on to the unspoken rules that one must follow in order even to engage another person in a simple conversation. Such deficits in social skills have been the focus of much interest for psychologists in recent years. And then there is the unfortunate individual whose learning ability seems absent when it comes to emotional relationships. One unhappy love affair follows another, and the same problems arise each time, becoming depressingly familiar. In fact all of us, if we are honest, can look at ourselves and find some problematic area of our social relations which the benefit of experience has not helped to change. Why don't we ever *learn*?

117

The kinds of answers that are on offer to these questions range from common sense through learning deficits to personality, and they are all fraught with problems. In the case of the persistent offender (whether adult or child) it seems self-evident simply from the point of view of common sense that punishment *should* (and therefore in most cases probably *does*) work. After all, we put ourselves in their shoes (so we think) and consider that the threat of imprisonment would be more than enough to make us stop and think before committing a crime. The logic of it is so persuasive, as is the apparent legitimacy of our own personal point of view (simply because it is our own) that we are left with the conclusion that such people are not rational beings (there's something wrong with the way they think), they are just plain 'bad' (there's something wrong with their personality) or they 'have no feelings', for neither themselves nor anyone else. The last explanation is often tied in with psychoanalytical concepts: for example, some 'hard-boiled' criminals have been referred to as suffering from 'affectionless psychopathy' (Bowlby, 1953), caused by a disrupted home life in their early years.

These explanations all bring problems in their wake. The notion of human beings as predisposed to irrational thought and behaviour is a terrifying one, and is not new. For example, Festinger's (1957) idea of 'cognitive dissonance' portrays us as manufacturers of rationalisations for our behaviour, rather than as rational decision makers. What faith can we place in our decision makers or ourselves if this is true? The other two types of explanation present problems for how we can ever improve the situation, since they are rooted in the traditional idea of personality (whether inherited genetically or formed in childhood) as stable, set and basically unchangeable.

Likewise, the individual whose love life always ends in disaster is likely to be seen as in some way emotionally inadequate (a personality deficit) and the person who is socially inept is seen as either 'shy' (a personality term which serves both as a description and an explanation) or as having failed to learn the appropriate cues, rules and behaviours for conversation. In the case of the latter problem, some hope of change is offered: if a person has failed to learn the correct behaviours, or has learned inappropriate ones, they can presumably be 'trained' in the skills they lack. Such 'social skills training' has become popular with psychologists and psychotherapists. Through the use of video recordings, role play and subsequent feedback, clients are taught to recognise their errors and to identify appropriate behaviour, for which they are rewarded by encouragement and approval from the trainer. Social skills training can be very helpful, but for some, who are otherwise intelligent people, it does not solve their problems. Sometimes they cannot 'transfer' their learning from the training context to real-life situations. It is often apparent that the problem for many of these people is not that they fail to recognise appropriate behaviours; they are quite as 'clued in' in this respect as those whom we would term socially competent. The problem lies in putting this knowledge into practice. So in a variety of ways, our usual explanations for why people 'never seem to learn' are fraught with problems themselves. Let us now look at these 'learning' difficulties and see what light a PCP approach can shed on them.

'Reward' and 'punishment' at first appear to be fairly straightforward ideas. In combination with a basically hedonistic 'pleasure principle' model of humankind, this recipe suggests, as we have already noted, that human beings will adopt behaviours that are rewarded and avoid those that are punished. Even within this behaviouristic model there are good reasons for doubting the efficacy of punishment as a shaper of human behaviour (see Skinner, 1974).

But the real problem is even more fundamental just what *is* a reward? What *is* a punishment? We should not have to enquire of many people before it became apparent that what is rewarding for one person is not so for another. Some strive for money, others for status or power. Some find their rewards in sex or friendship. For yet others it is food and drink. In the end, the only possible (and pragmatically useless) definition of a reward is 'that which a person finds rewarding'.

The same is true of punishment. For some, life on the proverbial desert island would be purgatory, for others heaven. The child who receives a caning on the behind for a misdemeanour may see it as the price you pay for popularity', 'proof of teachers' aggressive natures' or 'a sexual assault'.

In each of these cases it is obvious that the relationship between the punishment and subsequent behaviour is not a simple one. The point that we are making here is that events mean different things to different people (constructive alternativism). There are an infinite number of ways of construing (giving meaning to) an event, and it is dangerous to assume that our own construction (or even that adopted by many people, which is part of what we call 'common sense') is the right one. So in considering the effectiveness (or ineffectiveness) of reward and punishment, i.e. why people 'just don't learn, we have to recognise that it is the *meaning* that events hold for people, not the events themselves, which is the influential factor. Having said this, it may seem that what we are saying is that if we could just identify what is rewarding or punishing for any one person, we should hold the key to changing their behaviour, like Winston Smith in *1984*. But it is not as simple as this.

People can act only within a framework of possible choices open to them, and by this we do not just mean that people are limited by their circumstances (they may be disabled, poor or uneducated). Of course they are limited by these things in their capacity to change, but what matters is not the choices an outsider thinks are available to another person. People can change only if they themselves perceive that they have any options that make sense to them. Take, for example, a delinquent whose perspective on the world is dominated by a construct which continually asks 'Are you going to beat the system or let it beat you?'. For this person, criminal behaviour may bring with it undesirable side-effects (like imprisonment) but these are slight by comparison with the implications of what they perceive to be the only other choice available – being beaten by the system . So the choices we perceive to be available to us are always dependent upon the nature of our own construct system, the hue of the particular spectacles through which we have come to view the world. Looking at the problem in this way, it is obvious why notions such as 'learning', 'reward' and 'punishment' often do not serve us well when it comes to changing our (or other people's) behaviour. For the individual in the above example, change cannot come about until they have found a way of looking at life which does not entail the 'beat the system/be beaten by it' dichotomy. This may be a tall order, but at least it provides us with a more facilitative and optimistic view of human nature than those implied by either psychoanalytical or traditional personality theories.

Perceived choices and the nature of an individual's construing are also central, we would argue, to any real understanding of the other kinds of problems mentioned earlier in this chapter. For the person who cannot manage an ordinary conversation, or for the one who always seems to be making the same mistakes in their relationships, PCP can offer a better understanding of the problem than 'learning', and a more optimistic view of the future than 'personality'. Let us look at an example of what might be happening for a person who, in learning theory terms, has a social skills deficit.

Pauline had always thought of herself as a shy person. But unlike most people, after leaving behind the awkwardness of inexperience in adolescence, her social relationships deteriorated. She could often think of nothing to say for herself, and when she did speak (which was only when she was directly addressed) it was almost inaudible. She avoided eye contact with people, which made it even more difficult to hold a relaxed conversation with her, and her whole demeanour seemed to discourage interaction. She was at first enthusiastic when social skills training was suggested to her. The first few sessions went quite well, and she was quick to understand where her deficits lay. However, when it came to putting this knowledge into practice Pauline could make no progress. Role-play sessions were aimed at rewarding her for talking more, introducing topics of conversation and looking directly in the face of the person she was talking to. After one or two unsuccessful attempts she became depressed and requested that the sessions be terminated.

The key to Pauline's difficulties came to light when she was encouraged to talk about the difference, as she saw it, between herself and people who were 'good talkers' (the sort of person she was supposed to try to become). It seemed to her that the world could be divided up into people who are domineering and those who are sensitive. Domineering-sensitive was thus a construct which flavoured her approach to all social situations. In Kellian terms, this construct was superordinate for her because it played a very central role in how she thought about people, and because it tended to subsume other constructs, such as 'kind–cruel' and 'friendly–ruthless' (which also emerged as constructs characteristic of Pauline's thinking). The way she saw it, people who were confident in themselves and for whom smooth social interaction came easily gained their ability through their domineering and arrogant attitude. Basically, they were unself-conscious because they had no thought for other people. Those at the other end of the construct (which included herself) were sensitive, modest and caring. People like her, she realised, paid a price for their gentle nature (impossible social relations), but who in their right mind would want to become domineering, arrogant and thoughtless? The choice, as she perceived it, left her better off, though unhappy, at her end of the construct. The only way out for Pauline was to find a way for her to abandon her 'domineering–sensitive' construct in her thinking about people and replace it with an alternative that still allowed her to retain those aspects of herself she valued – sensitivity, caring, etc. but which could also accommodate 'good conversationalist'.

Kelly saw the way we use our constructs as rather like the way scientists use theories (he used the metaphor of 'person-as-scientist' as his model for human psychology). In Pauline's case, her (albeit unarticulated and implicit) theory was that people are either domineering or sensitive, and her experiences in social situations seemed to her to provide plenty of evidence to support her theory. Just as scientists sometimes have such an attachment to and belief in a particular theory that they may be less than impartial in their interpretation of the evidence (without consciously intending to 'fudge the data') so any one of us may have invested so heavily in a theory of ourselves and other people that we always find it being confirmed even when it is a theory, like Pauline's, that in the end makes us miserable. After all, who wouldn't sometimes rather be right than happy? It thus becomes obvious why so little progress was made when Pauline's difficulties were seen as a learning problem.

Another important point to realise is that the familiarity of running in the well-worn grooves of past thought and behaviour, even when it creates problems for us, sharply contrasts with the alternatives – striking out into new, and possibly dangerous, uncharted territory. Or even being unable to comprehend there being any alternative to our current ways of doing things. In the end, we tend to do the things we have always done, in the way we have always done them, even when we do them badly. We stick with what we know.

This helps us to make sense of the person's life that is a series of unsatisfactory and aborted relationships, and of the experience of many of us who see ourselves making the same mistakes within long-standing relationships. Over the years, the conflicts come to have a recognisably familiar theme, the same old issues are raised over and over, and each time we feel no better prepared to deal with them. We often feel ourselves precipitated into an unwanted replay of an old argument, and find ourselves unwillingly playing out the part we have always adopted. Why do we never learn? Surely the misery that results from such confrontations should be enough to teach us to do differently next time? Of course, what is really at the heart of this matter is not our learning ability but our construal of ourselves and our relationships, and either our reluctance to give up what we know how to do badly for an alternative which seems to us (like Pauline) to be worse, or our inability to envisage any other way of being. It is rather like trying to imagine what might lie beyond the limits of the universe.

> Marion was a person for whom, subjectively, relationships were about safeguarding her own interests at the expense of those of her 'opponents'. Although she was, she considered, otherwise happily married, over the eight years of her marriage the conflicts with her husband had begun to have the feel of a familiar ritual. It seemed to her that the perennial problem which cropped up regularly at holiday time, Christmas, social occasions, etc., was whether they did what *she* wanted or what he wanted. Either way, she was the loser, being left with feelings of either guilt or resentment, which marred her enjoyment of whatever they did in the end. Although she could see the damage it did and wished things could be different, on each occasion she felt she had to do the only thing she knew how to do – stake her claim, defend her corner. She knew several married friends who did not seem to have this particular problem, and yet, though she desperately wished to, was at a loss to understand how it was possible to see things in any other way. The repeated 'punishment' of marital discord, resentment and guilt did not help Marion to 'learn' to adopt a different approach to disagreements. Her 'tug-of-war' construal of relationships needed to be abandoned in favour of one in which 'winner versus loser' would not be an issue, and where compromise did not mean 'giving in'.

Just how great a task this would be for Marion depends upon how central or superordinate a place her 'winner versus loser' construct occupies in her construct system. The more superordinate the construct, the more fundamental and therefore threatening is the necessary change, and the greater the temptation to retreat to the unhappy safety of what is known and familiar.

Real personal change may never come about for some people. But the advantage of a PCP view of their problems is that it holds out to them the possibility of change and firmly identifies the agent of such change as the person him- or herself. It does not allow us to write off others or ourselves as 'bad characters', 'irrational' or 'sick', but urges us to endeavour to gain an understanding of their construal of their world, and of our own. This is the real launching pad of change.

Part V
Measurement and Change

In this final section we deal with the measurement and assessment of construct systems, and with personal change. Since most of the publications in PCP come from the pens of clinical psychologists and others engaged in the clinical field, much of what is written about these issues reflects this. The original focus of convenience for PCP was personal change, and thus *assessment* for such change is an integral part of this approach. The aim of this section is thus to demonstrate the methods and techniques that have grown out of PCP, and to show how they help us apply the principles of the theory to real-life problems.

In Chapter 19, we describe some of the most frequently used methods in PCP, linking them in with the key tenets of the theory. This is not a 'recipe-book' approach: our aim is not to provide the reader with a set of techniques which they can learn, like any practical skill, and which may be brought out and used on appropriate occasions; rather, the aim is to show how some of the principles of PCP have been applied, usually by clinicians, in real-life situations and also to bring out the limitations of measuring constructs. It is part of the intrinsic nature of construing that it is not amenable to quantification in the way that other psychologies are (and this is seen as a drawback of the theory by many psychologists).

In the final chapter of the book, we draw together the threads of the previous chapters and consider in detail what personal change means from a PCP standpoint. We take a look at what PCP psychotherapy entails, and how and why it differs in its approach from other psychotherapies.

Chapter 19
How Can We Measure Constructs?

In the worlds of academic and clinical psychology, PCP is better known for its methodology than its theory. In fact it is one aspect of its methodology, repertory grid technology, that is so well known, and almost has a life of its own. This is because it is a flexible technique that offers endless computational possibilities and perspectives combined with the seductive prospect of a sort of psychic X-ray. For many years, psychologists have been collecting repertory grid data and then subjecting them to sophisticated statistical treatment without fully understanding the mathematical assumptions they are buying into (Bell, 2003). They can mistakenly imagine that the computer printout gives them a privileged look at the exact workings of a person's mind. It is this misuse of the grid that highlights the danger in the question about the measurement of constructs. PCP proposes that a person's conduct can best be understood in the light of their theories, which are constituted by their constructs. But these theories and constructs do not really reside in people's heads, waiting for us to discover them. We cannot expect to uncover and measure them, as though they were physical entities. There is a danger in reifying constructs just as there is with traits and personality. Our language makes it all too easy to transform processes into structures, verbs into nouns. We question rather than 'have questions' and we construe rather than 'have constructs'.

All this might sound rather petty, but we must remember that the subtle tentacles of language readily paralyse thought. Kelly's dictum 'man is a form of motion' (1955: 48) bids us note that people are always doing something, engaged on some project or other. Human conduct is a mystery and it is best approached by asking what people are doing, how it reflects their construing. This is quite different from thinking that people have constructs that are in some way responsible for the way they act. In this latter formulation, the buck is passed to some fictional inner person, one that Gilbert Ryle called the 'ghost in the machine' (Ryle, 1949).

Having said all this, it is clearly important to attempt to understand a person's construing, and various techniques designed to do just this have evolved. We shall describe a few, and also use this opportunity to re-examine some of Kelly's propositions about the nature of construing. Students who wish to find out more about constructivist techniques of assessment should read Neimeyer (1993), DeNicolo (2003), Bell (2003) and Fransella, Bell and Bannister (2004).

The Role Construct Repertory Test

The Role Construct Repertory Test, or 'Rep. Test' reflects Kelly's simple definition of a construct – any way in which two things are alike and different from a third. Try it. Pick any three things, like a computer, a fire and a carpet. You might say that the computer is new, but you've had the other two for years. This points to a construct of new acquisitions versus old ones. There might be many constructs you could elicit from this triad (i.e. group of three things) and still more that other people would focus on. There are no right or wrong answers, just personally relevant dimensions along which things or events may be construed. Remember the question you might have been asked by a pupil in primary school: 'Which is the odd one out - dog, cat or radio? The cat, because you don't need a licence for it!' No one can deny the truth of this; it just seems like an irrelevant construct – except, maybe, to a licence collector! Clearly, a person could use an almost infinite number of such dimensions of construction, depending on what is being considered, the context. Every construct has a finite range of convenience, or ranges of elements (i.e. people or events) that it can sensibly be applied to. The construct 'need a licence versus don't' seems so trivial because of its very limited range compared with the comprehensive range of 'living creature versus inert'. One context that will be of universal importance is that concerning construing of people, and it was here that Kelly first devised the procedure. He gave his clients a role-title list comprising roles such as 'mother', 'self', 'best friend', 'husband'. 'a person you admire', etc. Using different triads they were then invited to elicit some bipolar constructs by suggesting ways in which two are alike and different from the third. This is not a psychological test as the term is usually understood, in which the psychologist assesses or scores what the client comes up with, and comes to conclusions based on statistical norms or professional judgements. The Kellian psychologist adopts a credulous approach in which the client's perspective is spelt out, elaborated and discussed. The aim is not to arrive at a tightly defined set of constructs, neatly pinned down to a set of verbal labels. We are not getting at a person's constructs, but looking at the way they construe. Two different people may use the same verbal labels to mean very different things, e.g. most people use the terms 'sensitive' or 'insensitive' at some time to describe others, and are likely to mean quite different things by them. What the psychologist and client do next depends on the task in hand. If nothing else at all is done, at least the point is made that everyone has a particular and valid outlook. Perhaps the client may be encouraged to investigate others' construing in the same or similar manner in an attempt to develop better communication with them. One thing that could be pursued is the meaning of constructs, since it is often our most important constructs that we find most difficult to put into words. This cannot be done by asking people and taking their answers at face value. Although Kelly's rule wherever possible was 'if you want to know what's wrong with someone, ask them – they may just tell you!', he recognised that people are not always in a position to do this. As we have already noted, language is often both ambiguous and inadequate at describing our meanings. A more satisfactory way of approaching meaning is by investigating the relationships between constructs, and their implications for each other. It was for this purpose that the repertory grid was devised.

The Repertory Grid

The repertory grid examines the relationships between constructs by comparing the way they apply to the same people or events (which are referred to as the 'elements' of the grid). Once the constructs have been elicited by whatever means (e.g. the Rep. Test) a grid is drawn up, with elements listed along the top and constructs listed down the side. There does not have to be any set number of columns or rows; they can be adjusted to suit the purpose of the grid. If, say, we were interested in the way a person construed people, we would obviously use people as the elements of the grid, and perhaps get as many constructs from the various triads available until the person felt that he or she had come up with all the important dimensions that they used in looking at people. At this stage, the grid could look something like Figure 19.1.

She or he would then be asked to consider each construct in turn, and say to which pole each element should be assigned. This may be done by using an X to denote the 'emergent' (left hand) pole, while an 0 denotes the 'contrast' (right hand) pole. The grid would now look something like Figure 19.2.

A cursory glance at the grid shows that, with only a few exceptions, the same people are considered to be both 'sensitive' and 'weak'. There is also a relationship between these two constructs and 'unattractiveness'. In grid terms, the meaning of any construct is defined in terms of its relationship

Constructs	Self	Mother	Best friend	A person I admire	Someone I dislike	Spouse	
				Elements			
Sensitive							Insensive
Friendly							Withdrawn
Weak							Strong
Not a risk taker							Adventurous
Practical							Creative
Unattractive							Attractive
Neat							Untidy

Figure 19.1 A repertory grid form.

× Constructs	Self	Mother	Best friend	A person I admire	Someone I dislike	Spouse	O
				Elements			
Sensitive	×	O	×	×	×	O	Insensive
Friendly	O	O	×	O	×	×	Withdrawn
Weak	×	O	×	O	×	O	Strong
Not a risk taker	O	O	×	O	O	×	Adventurous
Practical	×	×	O	×	O	O	Creative
Unattractive	×	O	×	O	×	O	Attractive
Neat	O	O	×	×	O	O	Untidy

Figure 19.2 A completed repertory grid.

with others, and thus to be sensitive implies that you are both weak and unattractive. Suppose that this was the grid of a man who was lonely and depressed, and had come to see the psychologist because his doctor felt that he would profit from social skills training. Part of this would involve training in sensitivity to others, watching and listening to them picking up their cues, perhaps reflecting their feelings and expressing affection when it is called for. We can predict from his grid that this man's construct system is likely to present him with problems in this area. From the therapist's point of view, sensitivity is a good thing, but not necessarily from the patient's! The therapist would be wise to take this into account before trying to show the patient how to act, exhorting him to be sensitive to others, etc. At the very least, an elaboration of the meaning of sensitivity is required first.

As an alternative to simply asking people to assign each element to one or other pole of each construct we might try to get them to make finer discriminations. We might ask them to rank the elements with respect to each construct from, say, the most sensitive to the least. Or we might ask them to apply a rating scale to each element. This would involve asking 'imagine a 7-point scale, where 1 = extremely sensitive and 7 = extremely insensitive. How would you rate this person on that scale?'. Both rankings and ratings provide more powerful data that can be used as the basis of a correlation coefficient and thus a more exact measure of construct relationships. Many computer programs exist that produce maps of whole construct systems based on such correlations. But these types of measure also require people to make very fine discriminations. Subtle nuances of meaning can be extracted from a matrix of figures that can be justified mathematically but not really psychologically. The delicacy and sophistication of the analysis can blind us to the relative coarseness of the data.

Nevertheless, the grid is a valuable technique capable of great flexibility and ingenuity. We can pick as elements anything that we want to get people's views on. The constructs that are used to evaluate music, bread, TV programmes, forms of exercise – all are open to elaboration through grid method, when elements to reflect the area of investigation can be selected accordingly. But its most reported use has been in the clinical field in which it was developed. In the following case study we can see how using social situations as the grid elements helps us to articulate a person's construing.

Suppose we have a client who has experienced panic in a range of situations that puzzles her. She can see no thread of similarity running through them, but can definitely divide them into those that pose a threat and those that do not. A fruitful line of investigation would be to devise a grid with elements made up of situations varying in threat. (Varying say, from being at home with her husband to shopping alone in a crowded supermarket.) Constructs could be elicited by comparing a series of pairs of elements, each pair made up of one safe and one threatening situation. The completion of a grid might well suggest 'active ingredients' in the constitution of panic. Again it must be emphasised that it is not for the psychologist to *interpret* the grid. It may well be the patient who, for the first time, spots and is able to verbalise exactly what it is that she fears, and where the danger lurks. As we have said, a person's emotions always have some meaning, they are never truly irrational. The grid can be a very effective key in unlocking this meaning. And of course, there is no need to confine elements to concrete situations or people. An element in a grid can be anything that we attempt to construe. It may be appropriate to focus on the way we see ourselves in different situations: panicky, eager to please, irritable and so on. Or perhaps we might develop Kelly's idea of a dependency grid (Kelly, 1955; Walker, 1997), in which the elements are situations, people or practices that we rely on when we are under some sort of pressure.

For a good introduction to grid method and its applications, the reader is referred to Fransella, Bell and Bannister (2004).

Laddering

One measure of importance of constructs is 'ordination'. PCP proposes that constructs are organised into a system where they have implications for each other. Relatively subordinate constructs have smaller ranges of convenience and consequently carry fewer implications for our lives. Imagine that you had elicited two constructs: has black hair versus blonde, and 'makes me tense' versus 'feel OK with'. The hair colour construct can be applied to only a very narrow range of events, whereas 'is he or she the sort that makes me tense?' is a question that the subject may ask of virtually everyone. Laddering is a technique devised to ascend a construct system from relatively subordinate to relatively superordinate constructs. One can also 'descend' the ladder to yet more subordinate constructs. (This is sometimes called *pyramiding*, since there may be several lines of descent.)

Suppose we started off wondering what the implications of a construct 'good mother versus selfish' were for a particular woman. We move up to superordinate constructs by asking 'why' questions. Having established that she would prefer to be at the 'good mother' end of the construct, we ask 'why?'. The ensuing conversation might reveal that in order for her to feel consistent with her image of herself as a caring, understanding person (as opposed to one who couldn't give a damn), it is vital to her that she be a good mother, whatever that means. And whatever it does mean can be approached by asking 'how' questions, thus moving down to the subordinate constructs. How can you tell if someone is a good mother? What counts as evidence? How does a good mother act, think, feel? When our subject replies that good mothers don't go out to work, don't lose their tempers, and always make time to play with their toddler, we begin to see why she is depressed! Some working mothers with demanding jobs will be able to reconcile their roles at work and home, but it will be no easy matter for this particular individual.

This laddering procedure is rarely as straightforward as it is portrayed here, and the lines up and down the construct system are not usually so apparent (Butt, 1995). Perhaps construct systems are not so neatly hierarchical after all. But certainly laddering can be an extremely fruitful style of interviewing. This is particularly so when people have difficulty in spelling out their idiosyncratic relationships in meaning. And of course core constructs, those most important superordinates which we use to define our identities, are often the most difficult for us to spell out. The rules they impose are so unquestionable and deviation from them so unthinkable that we rarely seriously consider living at the other end of the construct.

Getting people to spell out constructs that matter can be difficult, but in our example we can see why our woman is experiencing such guilt as she deviates from her core role.

Self-characterisation

This form of investigation nicely illustrates the point that we were making at the beginning of this chapter: that what we are interested in is looking at the way an individual construes, rather than the extraction of constructs. It is tempting, particularly for the researcher, to try to find neatly labeled constructs that can be analysed mathematically in grid form, even if these may represent a poor reflection of the individual's psychological processes. The self-characterisation offers no simple scoring methods, but it can give a rich picture of the way someone construes both themselves and their world. Consequently, it is a tool much favoured by PCP psychotherapists. The subject is asked: 'Write a character sketch of yourself, as though you were the principal character in a play. Write it from the point of view of someone who knows you intimately and sympathetically, perhaps better than anyone really could know you.' The sketch is not scored but, as Kelly says, 'brought into focus'. The whole exercise rests on that uniquely human ability to construe the constructions of others: to try to put yourself in someone else's shoes and see things through their eyes. Of course, the psychologist is not interested here in what others actually think, but what the client thinks they think. Self-constructions are ultimately based on the construing of the views of significant others. The instruction is geared to encourage you to paint an overall picture, yet one that is not superficial; while it is a 'sketch', it is written by another who knows you really well. You are not bidden to dwell on your faults, or what you ought to be like (it is written from a sympathetic point of view).

The product will inevitably bear the stamp of your core construing. Each writer has to choose what to focus on from an almost infinite variety of possibilities. Even if the result is a 6,000-word essay, you will not include everything that an actual observer would have included. And you will certainly approach things from an idiosyncratic perspective. Our basic position of constructive alternativism reminds us that there are many truths.

The facts do not speak for themselves; the narrator has to speak for them. We all have our own stories. We are historians, not chroniclers; we do not simply note 'what happens'; our theories alert us to certain themes and blind us to others. The art of reading a self-characterisation is to try to get into the perspective of the writer, and 'attempt a restatement of the argument', as Kelly puts it. Our own stories are written from a perspective that renders the perspective itself invisible. It is often through the tone and flavour of the sketch, rather than the content, that this may be evident. Alan Radley (1973) proposed that it is our core construing that constitutes this perspective. We can inspect and work with our subordinate constructs, but superordinate core constructs 'work us'. The therapist's job is to help us articulate and work on this core. (This is what Freud meant in saying 'where there is id, there shall be ego'.) In 'restating the argument', she or he attempts to reflect these core perspectives. This is not *interpretation*, but a process of *negotiation*; the subject/patient is always the final arbiter of what fits. The psychologist/ therapist has to put things propositionally: 'It looks to me like your slogan is something like "it's a vicious vindictive world, and my best bet is to appease it". Is that right?' Self-characterisations can be tailored to meet various needs. You could write one of 'me five years ago', or 'me when I get better'. If you are trying to decide whether to take a particular course of action, you could try two contrasting sketches of your future self, one as though you had and one as though you hadn't, say, taken a teacher-training course. It is important to realise that what you would get out of this is not what you will be like, or were like, but your view of it *now*. Perhaps, having crystallised this, it would help to discuss it with someone else. All these approaches to construing are forms of structuring conversation. A person's construing pervades everything they do – their dreams, their conversations, their posture. their clothes. Any interview can be used to.bring it into focus. Leitner (1985)'shows that core constructs can be elicited by talking to people about significant events such as early memories, fantasies, significant dreams, life-events, their philosophy of life and God, religion, and what they imagine will be a suitable epitaph for them. Working with metaphors such as Mair's 'community of self' (1977), as well as a variety of non-verbal methods might sometimes be the most suitable.

Systemic Bowties

This technique was devised by construct theorists working with families, or other such systems (Procter, 2003). The term 'systems' underlines how so much of our action is not simply an individual product, but involves anticipation of how others will act. After all, we are not hermetically sealed individuals, but actors who are always involved in dialogues and joint actions

with others. At the same time that others are trying to make sense of what
we do, we are doing the same with their action. What we intend by some
gesture or remark may very well not be the meaning that another person
takes from it. In systemic bowties, the therapist or researcher focuses on
what each participant is responding to and anticipating (in the therapeutic
situation, or in a problematic incident). So, one partner may say that she
never gets any sympathy from her partner; instead, he ignores her signals of
distress. He just comes home, then drinks and watches TV. But the other may
say that his partner doesn't realise the pressure he is under at work. It just
looks to him as though she sulks to make him feel guilty, and he refuses to be
'blackmailed' by her. So the 'bowtie' would look like this:

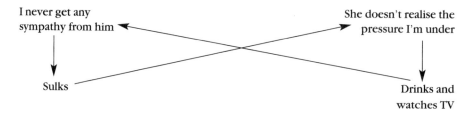

Figure 19.3 A systemic bowtie.

We can see how each person's construction is constantly validated by the
other's action and thus a sort of vicious circle is set up. The purpose of the
bowtie idea is to draw each participant's attention to this, and to underline
the principle of alternative constructivism; that there are always different
ways of making sense of the same thing. This might be obvious to the
constructivist, but it is not always clear to people in everyday life, where it is
often assumed that the way you see things is the way they are.

Throughout this chapter we have talked as though investigating our
construing is something we want to do. Reflecting on your life is in no way
necessary for a happy life; indeed, self-examination might lead to
unnecessary self-consciousness and problems. One thinks of the centipede
who never moved again after he wondered how he co-ordinated his legs! So
why and when do we want to examine our construing? Usually it is when
we are in some way dissatisfied with ourselves and want to change. Then,
standing back and examining our construing can be essential to working
with our constructions rather than being worked by them. PCP's original
focus was in the project of psychological reconstruction, and it is this to
which we turn in our final chapter.

Chapter 20
How Can I Change?

In the preface, we emphasised that this book was not to be considered a self-help book. This is because self-help manuals are typically written in a 'how-you-do-it' style. Human conduct is seen either in terms of unfortunate habits that we can discard with enough determination and practice, or skills that we can acquire by similar means. We repeatedly fail to keep our New Year's resolutions, but hope that psychology can give us a new and less painful route towards the same ends. The cognitive–behavioural approach that lies behind most self-help books accepts this sort of formulation of problems: 'so you want to give up smoking/stand up for yourself/ be more attractive to others? ... then try these exercises.'

It should be very clear by now that PCP takes a radically different view of our problems. We expect there to be many a difficulty in erasing an old behaviour or putting on a new one over our existing psychological clothes. All behaviour, whether old or new, has some function within a person's construct system, and we should expect a degree of disturbance in the course of behaviour change in proportion to the implications for the rest of the system. Subordinate change will cause fewer ripples within a system than superordinate change. Changing core construing, those constructs through which we define our selves and identities, will be the most difficult of all. Butt and Bannister (1987) looked at people who had not been helped by social skills training, a behavioural approach that teaches assertiveness as though it were a skill. They identify the main drawback of the skills analogy as its assumption that the execution of the skilled behaviour will carry no problem implications for the person. If you learn to type, it is an uncomplicated asset; once you couldn't do it, now you can. The opposite of the skilled behaviour is the nothing that you did before. But assertiveness is not a skill in this sense. Not standing up for yourself is not just the absence of something; it is a way of conducting yourself in public. Other people are going to be surprised when you change. At the very least, you are going to lead less of a quiet life, and your self-theory is probably going to need comprehensive revision. We are always doing something, although it may not be at all clear to us exactly what it is. Perhaps we are being 'friendly and sociable', and being assertive looks like violating this core role, no matter what the therapist thinks about it. So, from our point of view, change is not just a matter of 'how' questions, but also 'what' and 'why' questions. No therapist or counsellor can take a client's request for change entirely at face value; there has to be a negotiation focusing on what is realistic, what might be the unintended consequences of change, and what the relative costs and benefits are. Bannister (1975) emphasised that when people seek therapy, they are likely to frame their problem and phrase their request in ways that are unhelpful. Had their construing of their problem been of any use, they would probably have come up with some answers already. The first task in therapy has to be to examine alternative constructions of the problem: in Don Bannister's words, 'to take a walk round the psychological landscape'. In our view, no self-help book can provide all the answers to the reader's ready-formed questions. The first step must be to examine critically the questions. If this book has done nothing else, it has surely underlined the fact that our questions often need reviewing!

So in any change programme, there should be a process of finding out where we want to go before we try to get there.

Knowing What We Want

Any change involves choice. We often discover that the change that we would like will come only as part of a package deal which we had not bargained on and are not prepared for. It follows that there is a sense in which we do not really know what we want. By this we certainly do not mean that the psychologist or the therapist knows best; but we should do well to ponder on all the possible ramifications of a course of action before we embark on it. At least we should not be surprised or disheartened if we have a chance to grasp an opportunity only to find that it does not represent something we wanted after all. A marriage or a divorce, a new job or retirement, a new car or dress – how often have we found that they are not the answer to our problems after all. Stefan (1977) reported an experiment he carried out in which students were asked to act the role of 'good student' over a period of time. This involved carrying out various actions typically thought to constitute the role. He had predicted that they would come to embrace the role and feel themselves to be at home in it, due to the strong positive reinforcement they would encounter of their new behaviour. The results showed quite the reverse. Students felt more distanced from the roles they had enacted, and it did not matter how much their own view of what constituted a good student differed from the role that they had enacted. In subsequent interviews, Stefan found that students had found out something about what a realistic aim was for them through the enactment. Even those whose personal ideals had matched the 'good student' role found that the actions comprising the role caused too many ripples in their lives. Being a good student seemed attractive, but asking questions, reading in libraries, etc. did not have the same appeal! It was not just that this entailed harder work, it also called for more explanations to others.

So ideally we should know where we want to go before we try to go there, but quite often we find out only en route. In fact, it is asking too much of ourselves that we always foresee and understand the implications of our plans. Trying things out, experimenting, is the way people usually do find out what they want. Of course, it's easier to find out what you don't want than what you do, and it is when people feel stuck – being unhappy with where they are now yet not knowing which way to turn that they might seek the help of a therapist.

PCP Psychotherapy

In this section, we shall describe some of the strategies and tactics that a therapist using constructivist principles might employ (the terms *some* and *might* are used advisedly here). A personal construct psychologist would be defined by the approach he or she took to personal problems and not by any box of tricks he or she might use. In this book we have tried to spell out this approach and, where appropriate, contrast it with those characteristics or other approaches to personality. The constructivist way of construing will recommend appropriate techniques, many from other therapists' tool bags. So the therapist's approach is theory driven, but the therapist is technically eclectic. He or she will use a variety of techniques that were originally devised by therapists of other schools, say psychoanalysts and behaviour therapists. This makes the orienting theoretical approach all the more important, as it will inform everything that the therapist does. Just as there are many ways of preparing and serving up potatoes, so there are to using a particular therapeutic technique, say dream analysis or role play. What matters is the context and the flavour, the use to which the technique is put, the job it has to do.

As we have stressed, it is always useful to think about contrasts in order to help us define the important features of an approach. The contrast to constructivist thought in general, and therapy in particular, may be thought of as 'objectivist'. Psychiatric, cognitive-behavioural and psychoanalytic therapies may all be thought of as objectivist. They all try to objectively define both psychological health and psychological disorders. Then they attempt to help people move from one position to the other. Consequently, they are somewhat prescriptive and normative. From a constructivist point of view, they underplay the way in which the person is a product of both social and personal construction. So, according to the Diagnostic and Statistical Manual for Mental Disorders (DSM), homosexuality was classified as a mental illness until 1974. Then in the wake of changes in society, it ceased to be classified as such. Up until then, lesbianism and pedophilia would both be grouped as sexual perversions as though this was an objectively verified scientific truth. Therapists would accordingly 'help' people to change their sexual orientation towards an acceptable norm. Many of these therapists were liberal-minded professionals with no particular prejudice against gay people. But they subscribed to an objectivist theory of knowledge that believed that scientific truths were simply discovered, and not in any way constructions. In contrast, constructivists would recognise both a discovered and a constructed aspect to psychological disorder: there are always alternative constructions, and some are better than others.

As Neimeyer and Baldwin (2003) point out, Kelly was a constructivist pioneer, but there is now an extended family of constructivist therapies in the field. The influence of Kelly and others in individual therapy, and social constructionism (See Burr, 2003) in family therapy have produced what they term a loose confederation of approaches that share a lot of common ground. All see the person if not as a scientist (this is particular to Kelly's theory), then as an active meaning-maker who acts in the light of the particular constructions that he or she has put together. They emphasise how individuals produce narratives about their experience and that it is these personal stories, rather than what has actually happened to us, that shapes our action. What orthodox, objectivist accounts see as 'symptoms' of disorder are best seen as strategies adopted in line with a person's processes of construction. The therapist's task is to encourage more useful constructions and to co-author new narratives.

Bannister (1983) suggested that therapists call on a variety of implicit metaphors in their relationships with clients. These then impose a shape on the type of interaction and dialogue possible. He proposes that the psychoanalytic relationship is a mixture of doctor/patient and priest/penitent, while behaviour therapy conjures up trainer/trainee and client-centred psychotherapy friend/friend. The construct psychotherapist strives for research supervisor/research student as the ideal therapeutic relationship (See Chapter 11).

This metaphor recognises that the client retains ultimate control, knowing more about the project, its aims, its history, and its current status. The supervisor's expertise is in a more general area, advising on realistic objectives, methods of putting things to the test, and how to draw valid conclusions. Students often approach a supervisor with very vague ideas, and the first task is to help the student to frame an answerable question. A client may want to know how to feel less anxious with people, or how to be less depressed, but the therapist has no magic wand with which to bring this about. To a construct psychotherapist, these feelings are there for a reason, they say something about the client's life and experience. They are not just emotions that can be wiped away. Of course, they can be so crippling that something needs to be done to alleviate them, but in the long run their meaning cannot be ignored. Perhaps they will be resolved by questions such as 'How can I deal with my husband differently?' or 'What can I do about feeling anxious when I always suspect that I'm being watched by a very critical and unfriendly audience?'. As we emphasised in Part IV, this is perhaps the most important phase of either research or therapy. It is more useful to put in a bit of thought and work at this stage than to just launch into some course and 'see what happens'. What you put into a project determines what you get out, and mindless activity begets meaningless results. But some sort of investigation has to issue from all this. The client/researcher must attempt to get some answers to his or her questions, otherwise therapy and research would be nothing more than armchair philosophy.

This first stage of therapy involves what Kelly called the *loosening* of constructs. The client is encouraged to cast off from old and cherished perspectives, become a constructive alternativist, and look for new angles on the problem. This, then, has to be complemented by *tightening*, in which things are tried out and the value of new constructions put to the test. Therapy might comprise more than one cycle of loosening and tightening but Kelly was insistent that both are necessary to successful construct change. Some forms of therapy emphasise one aspect of the cycle at the expense of the other, but a construct therapist believes that both reflection and resolve, dreaming and action, complement each other in the quest for psychological change.

Once the tightening, experimental stage of the project is underway, the supervisor can advise on how to procede. He or she has seen similar (but not identical) projects, has a rough idea of what sort of approach might be of use, and knows that any project comprises 5% inspiration and 95% perspiration, that students often bite off more than they can chew and then become disheartened, and that any experiment needs careful thought and planning.

PCP indicates that it is easier to work on subordinate than on superordinate constructs. Although clients often want change in core constructs, this will occasion threat and guilt if this is attempted too quickly. Bannister (1975) likens therapeutic change to the task of repairing a ship at sea; the job might be completed by gradually replacing planks, but to attempt to strip out the keel straight away would be to invite disaster. No one can afford to be rudderless in a stormy sea.

When we consider the possible sites of change experiments, the role of the therapeutic relationship is pivotal. One very important dimension along which different therapies vary is the extent to which they see reconstruction being born in the therapy sessions. At one end we have both the psychoanalysts and the Rogerians, who see the therapy hour as the crucible of change. This rests on their assumption that any psychological problem of any moment will have its origins in important personal relationships. The theory is that in early life, each person develops strategies for dealing with the inevitable pain and conflict arising in the course of relationships with powerful and important others. These first relationships (termed 'object relations' by the analysts) also provide a model for those significant others later in life on to whom we transfer the perceptions and expectations which were appropriate in the past, but may be highly damaging now. It follows from this logic that the necessary insight and relearning has to take place in the context of a special type of important personal relationship.

Psychoanalysis attempts to create a climate in which the analyst tries to pick up the client's transferences (the inappropriate perceptions and expectations) which are then interpreted. The aim is to help the client undergo a corrective emotional experience in which he or she is gradually able to develop new styles of relationship. Only then are links made with relationships in the outside world and in the past. Humanists like Rogers (1961) also see the active ingredient of psychotherapy as the therapeutic relationship. They too see neurotic disturbance as resulting from childhood experiences (such as rejection) in the face of which the child has had to devise various defensive manoeuvres. Healing comes not so much from the therapist's techniques as from his or her personality; it is their non-possessive warmth, genuineness and empathy that provides the corrective experience, again in the therapy hour. At the other end of the spectrum we have the 'trainer/ trainee' model of the cognitive-behaviour therapists. Here, the client's progress depends on what happens outside the therapy hour, and the therapist's task is to provide the information and skills necessary for the successful execution of target behaviours and homework assignments. Whether dealing in skills of assertive behaviour or 'rational thinking' (see Ellis and Harper, 1975), the therapist attempts to empower the client to confront the obstacles encountered in everyday life. The therapy hour takes the form of a report-back session with encouragement, rehearsal, and planning of future goals.

Like the cognitive behaviourist, the construct psychologist does not assume that early object relations are the root of all problems. The therapeutic relationship might possibly provide the best or only weapon in the battle for change, but there is absolutely no reason why this should be the case. Clearly there is an important truth in the observation that early non-verbal construing can, and indeed does, sometimes play havoc in our subsequent encounters. But this is no reason to restrict the therapeutic armoury to one weapon to be trundled out on every occasion. Nevertheless, Leitner and his colleagues (Leitner and Thomas, 2003) stress the importance for all people of achieving intimacy in role relationships. In what they term 'experiential personal construct psychotherapy', the therapist uses transference and counter-transference in order to get the client to engage in, rather than retreat from, satisfying role relationships. For personal construct theorists, role relationships are those where the person is engaged in truly understanding the other's constructions. We may, however, adopt the strategy of retreating from such intimacy when it has resulted for us in the invalidation of our own core construing. A life of safe but impoverished relating is the result, and the experiential variant of personal construct therapy focuses on encouraging the client to re-engage through the use of transference relationships in therapy.

Generally, constructivist therapists would agree with the cognitive behaviourists that therapy is essentially an educational enterprise. But the research supervisor is no trainer: the trainer has a clear end product in view, knows what effective social behaviour looks like and what constitutes rational thinking; the construct therapist's credo, on the other hand, is that everything clients do is rational from their point of view, and is in some sense 'effective'. There is more to education than training, and there is nothing to be gained from trying to train the client in accordance with someone else's prescription of what is rational and effective. To educate literally means 'to lead out', and this is the research supervisor's aim: to work from the client's aims and perspective to help her with her project.

Of course, every metaphor has its limits of application. The 'supervisor' metaphor nicely captures the spirit of construct psychotherapy, its democratic intention. But we must beware of taking it too literally. The analogy has difficulty in encompassing those therapeutic manoeuvres which, as in psychoanalysis, are focused in the therapeutic relationship. This focus is indicated when a client's best opportunity for experiment appears to be with the therapist. As we have already said, this is the preferred site of operations for the psychoanalyst and the experiential therapist, where the transference is seen as the only true indicator of superordinate problems as well as presenting the most potent possibilities for solutions.

The personal construct therapist does not dive into the transference in preference to other waters, but recognises that unique opportunities are offered by looking at and working with the conduct in the therapy session itself. A client may say that people he meets act aggressively towards him despite his obvious and open vulnerability. The therapist may find his account of his innocence in these interactions hard to accept, given his habitual truculence in sessions. Their attitude is not one of disbelief, but of sceptical questioning. They form the hypothesis that the client typically adopts a rather aggressive stance to others, perhaps as a defence to forestall his expectation of rejection. The client's attitude is apparent in a range of non-verbal signals that unintentionally invite confrontation. If the therapist is correct, he will have great difficulty in overcoming his shyness as long as he frames the problem in terms of other people's aggression. He needs to experiment with his own behaviour, but first he must see this as an issue. This is where the therapist can raise her impression of the client as evidence of the hypothesis. The art of therapy, of course, is making such observations in such a way that they are not seen as challenges to be rejected out of hand. Skillfully handled, such an encounter can be a pivotal point in therapy, provided that it represents a valid perspective on events that the client is able to entertain and, ultimately, use.

In order to capitalise fully on a transference interpretation, a psychoanalyst would comment not only on the client's behaviour (aggression), but also on the feeling (perhaps vulnerability) against which it was designed to defend. Furthermore, when possible, he or she would link the pattern to early object relations. Kelly pointed out that, strictly speaking, the therapist never interprets; it is always the client who does the interpreting. The therapist suggests a construction, and any power it comes to have will depend on what the client can make out of it. The therapist's job is to help the client reconstrue, but in the end it is the client's project, it is he or she who has to reconstrue. The therapist is a teacher, but the teacher cannot do the learning for the student. The analyst's 'intepretations' must be couched in terms that the client can make sense of. It is the client who is the final arbiter of the truth.

Interplay with the therapist is one of two ways in which experimentation is brought into the therapy room. The other is via role play or, as Kelly termed it, 'enactment'. Here, the client is encouraged to explore alternative constructions through taking the roles of others. At its most modest, it might involve the client adopting the role of, say, a friend talking to the therapist about the client for a couple of minutes. At the most ambitious end of the spectrum is fixed-role therapy (Kelly, 1955; Bannister, 1975; Epting, 1984).

Although fixed-role therapy is a technique specific to personal construct psychotherapy, this does not mean that it is always used by the construct therapist: far from it. It is a demanding strategy that is normally resorted to only when therapy is stuck and the client is having great difficulty in experimenting. It involves the client attempting to act a part sketched out for him or her by the therapist. Following careful reading of the client's self-characterisation, the therapist (preferably in conjunction with other construct psychologists) draws up a sketch of an imaginary person, based on constructs 'oblique' to those used by the client. For example, if she sees herself as being either at war with her husband or being a 'good little wife' to him, the therapist may base the fixed role on a woman who is predominantly independent and considerate. The idea of acting this new person is not that the client should aim at becoming like her; it is in no sense an ideal. It would be entirely unrealistic to expect anyone to be able to change long term habits as the result of a spell of play-acting. The aim, as with any other Kellian enactment, is that the client is given the opportunity to try out a new perspective with the protection of make-believe. We have seen that PCP emphasises the threat involved in any hint of change in core role. Make-believe offers a cloak under which a person can try on some new clothes with absolutely no obligation to buy. Hypnosis allows similar experimenting, where the 'trance state' gives permission for new conduct and experience (Burr and Butt, 1989).

The fixed role is written to include both major and minor experiments, though care is taken not to be too prescriptive. The client has to be free to flesh out the role in ways that seem plausible to him or her and is consulted on the viability of the new character before any enactment begins. Once it does commence, it may be wise for the role to be introduced in a gradient of situations, starting with those that carry little penalty for embarrassment before proceeding to others which are more challenging. So it will be easier to do your shopping in a new role than to play it with your parents.

The experiment is normally continued for a finite period of, say, two to three weeks, during which time therapeutic sessions occur more frequently, to monitor progress. It does not matter just how good a 'performance' the client manages. This is not a rehearsal for an act to convince anyone else; it is an experiment with perspectives. In Bannister's words, the client is inveigled into recognising that personality is an invention (Bannister, 1975). The hope is that where the client felt entrapped, they might sense freedom; where they saw only tight circles of repetitive behaviour, they might glimpse a way of achieving escape velocity.

What then, is the end point of therapy? Of course, there is no simple answer to this. We can approach this, our final conundrum, however, by asserting that it is *not* happiness. No therapy can dissolve life's obstacles, pitfalls and conflicts. We concur with Kovel's criticism (1976) of those therapies that appear to offer some sort of personal growth as proof against life's tragedies. Kelly (1955) cautions therapists to beware of clients who are in search of 'peace of mind they consider to be synonymous with a monastic unconcern for human problems in the flesh'. The change we *can* legitimately pursue is in the way we construe life events. 'Construe' means not only 'look at' but also 'deal with'. Reconstruction is hard work and the change we get may not be the change we bargained for. The first step in reconstruction is to trade in some of our old questions for new ones.

Further Reading
and References

Further reading

This book has been written as an *invitation* to PCP rather than an *introduction* to it. Its aim has been to raise questions in the readers' minds, and whet their appetites for this approach to personality. For those who would like to explore further, there are several possible places to begin.

Fay Fransella's *International Handbook of Personal Construct Psychology* (Chichester: Wiley, 2003), is an excellent book to start with. It is an edited collection to which most prominent constructivists have contributed 4,000-word chapters. It is comprehensive in its coverage, written in plain English, and is an excellent account of the state of the approach at the turn of century.

Don Bannister and Fay Fransella's *Inquiring Man* (London: Penguin, 1971) is probably the best short introduction to personal construct psychology. It has just been produced as an electronic book.

The Internet Encyclopaedia of PCP is a new electronic resource. It includes definitions and elaborations of the terms and concepts of personal construct psychology. http://www.pcp-net.de/encyclopaedia

Works of George Kelly

Kelly, G. A. (1955/1991) *The Psychology of Personal Constructs*. Two volumes. First published by Norton: New York, 1955, then by Routledge in collaboration with the Centre for Personal Construct Psychology, 1991.

Kelly, G. A. (1963) *A Theory of Personality* (The first three chapters of The Psychology of Personal Constructs). New York: Norton.

Maher, B. (1969) (Ed) Clinical Psychology and Personality: The Selected Papers of George Kelly. New York: Wiley.

General

The *Journal of Constructivist Psychology* is published quarterly by Taylor and Francis

Butt, T. W. (2003) Understanding People. Basingstoke: Palgrave McMillan

Fransella, F. and Dalton, P. (2000) Personal Construct Counselling in Action (2nd edition) London: Sage.

Fransella, F. (1995) George Kelly. London: Sage.

Fransella, F., Bell, R. and Bannister, D. (2004) *A Manual for Repertory Grid Technique* (2nd edition). Chichester: Wiley.

Green, D. and Butler, R. (1998) *The Child Within: The Exploration of Personal Construct Theory with Young People*. Oxford: Butterworth-Heinemann.

Neimeyer, G. J. (1993) (ed) *Constructivist Assessment: A Casebook*. London: Sage.

Neimeyer, R. A. and Raskin, J. (2000) *Constructions of Disorder: Meaning Making Frameworks for Psychotherapy*. Washington, DC: American Psychological Association.

Neimeyer, R. A. (2002) *Lessons of Loss: A Guide to Coping* (2nd .edition) New York: Brunner Routledge.

Pope, M. and DeNicolo, P. (2001) *Transformative Education: Personal Construct Approaches to Practice and Research*. London: Whurr.

Ravenette, A. T. (1999) *Personal Construct Theory in Educational Psychology: A Practitioner's View*. London: Whurr.

Winter, D. (1992) *Personal Construct Psychology in Clinical Practice*. London: Routledge.

Electronic resources

Two new electronic resources are available on the www:

A new electronic journal, *Personal Construct Theory and Practice* contains articles and book reviews focusing on PCP: http://www.pcp-net.org/journal/

The Internet Encyclopaedia of PCP has entries covering all aspects of the approach that have been provided by scholars in the field: http://www.pcp-net.org/encyclopaedia

References

Bannister, D. (1975). *Issues and Approaches in the Psychological Therapies*. Chichester: Wiley.

Bannister, D. (1983). The internal politics of psychotherapy. In: Pilgrim, D. (Ed.) *Psychology and Psychotherapy*, pp. 139–150. London: Routledge.

Bell, R, (2003) Repetory grid technique. In: F. Fransella (Ed) *International Handbook of Personal Construct Psychology*, pp. 95–103. Chichester: Wiley.

Bowlby, J. (1953). *Child Care and the Growth of Love*. London: Penguin.

Breuer, J. and Freud, S. (1984). Studies on hysteria (1893–1895). Vol. II of the The *Standard Edition of the Complete Works of Sigmund Freud*. London: Hogarth Press, 1955.

Burr, V. and Butt, T. (1989). A personal construct view of hypnosis. *British Journal of Experimental and Clinical Hypnosis* 6, 85–90.

Burr, V. (2003) *Introduction to Social Constructionism* (Second edition). London; Routledge.

Butt,T. and Bannister, D. (1987). Better the devil you know. In: Dryden, W. (Ed.) *Key Cases in Psychotherapy*, pp. 127–147. London: Croom Helm.

Butt, T. W. (1995) The ordinal relationship between constructs. *Journal of Constructivist Psychology* 8, 227–236

Carr, E.H. (1961). *What is History?* London: Penguin.

DeNicolo, P. (2003) Elicitation methods to fit different purposes. In: F. Fransella (Ed) *International Handbook of Personal Construct Psychology*, pp. 123–131. Chichester: Wiley.

Ellis, A. and Harper, R. (1975). *A New Guide to Rational Living*. Hollywood: Wilshire Books.

Epting, F. (1984). *Personal Construct Counselling and Psychotherapy*. Chichester: Wiley.

Festinger, L. (1957). *A Theory of Cognitive Dissonance*. Stanford, Calif: Stanford University Press.

Foucault, M. (1981) *The History of Sexuality: Volume 1*. Harmondsworth: Penguin.

Fransella, F., Bell, R. and Bannister, D. (2004). *A Manual for Repertory Grid Technique* (2nd. Edition) Chichester: Wiley.

Gergen, K. J. and Gergen, M. M. (1984) The social construction of narrative accounts. In Gergen K. J. and Gergen M.M. (Eds) *Historical Social Psychology*. Hillsdale, NJ: Lawrence Erlbaum Associates.

Harré R. & Gillett, G. (1994) *The Discursive Mind*. London: Sage.

Heather, N. and Robertson, I. (1986). *Problem Drinking*. London: Penguin.

Kelly, G. (1955). *The Psychology of Personal Constructs*. New York: Norton.

Kovel, J. (1976). *A Complete Guide to Therapy*. Penguin.

Leitner, L. (1985). Interview methodologies for construct elicitation. In: Epting, F. and Landfield, A. (Eds) *Anticipating Personal Construct Psychology*, pp. 292-305. Lincoln Nebr: University of Nebraska Press.

Leitner, L. and Thomas, J. (2003) Experiential personal construct psychotherapy. In: F. Fransella (Ed) *International Handbook of Personal Construct Psychology*, pp. 257-264. Chichester: Wiley.

Mahoney, M. (1974). *Cognition and Behaviour Modification*. Cambridge, Mass: Ballinger.

Mahoney, M. J. (1991) *Human Change Processes*. New York: Basic.

Mair, J.M.M. (1977). The community of self. In: Bannister, D. (Ed) *New Perspectives in Personal Construct Theory*, pp. 125-151. London: Academic Press.

Neimeyer, G. J. (1993) (Ed) *Constructivist Assessment: A Casebook*. London: Sage.

Neimeyer, R. A. (2002) *Lessons of Loss: A Guide to Coping* (2nd. Edition) New York: Brunner Routledge.

Neimeyer, R. A. and Baldwin, S. A. (2003) personal construct psychotherapy and the constructivist horizon. In: F. Fransella (Ed) *International Handbook of Personal Construct Psychology*, pp. 247-255. Chichester: Wiley.

Plummer, K. (1975). *Sexual Stigma*. London: Routledge.

Plummer, K. (1995) *Telling Sexual Stories: Power, Change and Social Worlds*. London: Routledge.

Procter, H. (2003) Family therapy. In: F. Fransella (Ed) *International Handbook of Personal Construct Psychology*, pp.431-438. Chichester: Wiley.

Radley, A. (1973). *A study of self-elaboration through role change*. Unpublished PhD thesis, University of London.

Rogers, C. (1961). *On Becoming a Person*. London: Constable Press.

Ryle, G. (1949) *The Concept of Mind*. London: Hutchinson

Salmon, P. (1985). *Living in Time*. London: Dent.

Sarbin, T. (1986). The narrative as a root metaphor for psychology. In: Sarbin, T. (Ed.) *Narrative Psychology: The Storied Nature of Human Conduct*, pp. 3-21. London: Praeger.

Schacter, S. and Singer, J. (1962). Cognitive, social and psychological determinants of emotional state. *Psychological Review* 69, 379-399.

Sewell, K. W. (1997) Post-traumatic stress: Towards a constructivist model of psychotherapy. In: G. J. Neimeyer & R. A. Neimeyer (Eds.) *Advances in Personal Construct Psychology, Volume 4*, pp. 207-235.

Sewell, K. W. (2003) An approach to post-traumatic stress. In: F. Fransella (Ed) *International Handbook of Personal Construct Psychology*, pp. 223-231. Chichester: Wiley.

Sewell, K. W., Cromwell, R.L., Farrell-Higgins, J., Ohlde, C., and Patterson, T. W. (1996) Hierarchical elaboration in the conceptual structure of Vietnam combat veterans. . *Journal of Constructivist Psychology* 9, 79–96.

Skinner, B.F. (1974). *About Behaviourism*. New York: Vintage Books.

Stefan, C. (1977) Core structure theory and implications. In: Bannister, D. (Ed.) *New Perspectives in Personal Construct Theory*, pp. 281–299. London: Academic Press.

Storr, A. (1979). *The Art of Psychotherapy*. London: Secker and Warburg.

Tschudi, F. (1977). Loaded and honest questions. In: Bannister, D. (Ed.) *New Perspectives in Personal Construct Theory*, pp. 321–351. London: Academic Press.

Walker, B. (1997) Shaking the kaleidoscope: Dispersion of dependency and its relationships. In: G. J. Neimeyer and R. A. Neimeyer (Eds.) *Advances in Personal Construct Psychology, Volume 4*, pp.63-97.

Weeks, J. (1986). *Sexuality*. London: Tavistock.

Winter, D. (2003) Psychological disorder as imbalance. In: F. Fransella (Ed) *International Handbook of Personal Construct Psychology*, pp.201-209. Chichester: Wiley.

Index